JAMES
BECKWOURTH

JAMES BECKWOURTH

Sean Dolan

Senior Consulting Editor
Nathan Irvin Huggins
Director
W.E.B. Du Bois Institute for Afro-American Research
Harvard University

CHELSEA HOUSE PUBLISHERS
New York   Philadelphia

CHELSEA HOUSE PUBLISHERS
Editor-in-Chief Richard S. Papale
Managing Editor Karyn Gullen Browne
Copy Chief Philip Koslow
Picture Editor Adrian G. Allen
Art Director Maria Epes
Assistant Art Director Howard Brotman
Manufacturing Director Gerald Levine
Systems Manager Lindsey Ottman
Production Manager Joseph Romano
Production Coordinator Marie Claire Cebrián

Black Americans of Achievement
Senior Editor Richard Rennert

Staff for JAMES BECKWOURTH
Copy Editor Ian Wilker
Editorial Assistant Michele Berezansky
Designer Diana Blume
Picture Researcher Nisa Rauchenberg
Cover Illustration Steven Sullivan

First Printing

1 3 5 7 9 8 6 4 2

Library of Congress Cataloging-in-Publication Data
Dolan, Sean.
    James Beckwourth, frontiersman/by Sean Dolan
      p. cm.
      Includes bibliographical references and index.
    Summary: Examines the life and career of the nineteenth-century
hunter, trapper, and trader.
    ISBN 0-7910-1120-8.
        0-7910-1285-9 (pbk.)
    1. Beckwourth, James Pierson, 1798–1866—Juvenile literature. 2.
Pioneers—West (U. S.)—Biography—Juvenile literature. 3. West
(U. S.)—Biography—Juvenile literature. 4. Trappers—West
(U.S.)—Biography—Juvenile literature. [1. Beckwourth, James
Pierson, 1798–1866. 2. Pioneers. 3. Afro-Americans—Biography.]
I. Title.
F592.B393D65 1992   91-33274
978'.302'092—dc20   CIP
[B]   AC

Frontispiece: Among the Sierra
Nevada Mountains, California,
by Albert Bierstadt, the first major
American artist to depict the West.
Bierstadt painted this scene in 1868,
almost two decades after James
Beckwourth discovered an important
pass through the mountains in
northern California, a few miles
northwest of present-day Reno,
Nevada.

CONTENTS

————— ❧ —————

BLACK AMERICANS OF ACHIEVEMENT

HANK AARON
baseball great

KAREEM ABDUL-JABBAR
basketball great

RALPH ABERNATHY
civil rights leader

ALVIN AILEY
choreographer

MUHAMMAD ALI
heavyweight champion

RICHARD ALLEN
*religious leader and
social activist*

MAYA ANGELOU
author

LOUIS ARMSTRONG
musician

ARTHUR ASHE
tennis great

JOSEPHINE BAKER
entertainer

JAMES BALDWIN
author

BENJAMIN BANNEKER
scientist and mathematician

AMIRI BARAKA
poet and playwright

COUNT BASIE
bandleader and composer

ROMARE BEARDEN
artist

JAMES BECKWOURTH
frontiersman

MARY MCLEOD BETHUNE
educator

JULIAN BOND
civil rights leader and politician

GWENDOLYN BROOKS
poet

JIM BROWN
football great

BLANCHE BRUCE
politician

RALPH BUNCHE
diplomat

STOKELY CARMICHAEL
civil rights leader

GEORGE WASHINGTON
CARVER
botanist

RAY CHARLES
musician

CHARLES CHESNUTT
author

JOHN COLTRANE
musician

BILL COSBY
entertainer

PAUL CUFFE
merchant and abolitionist

COUNTEE CULLEN
poet

ANGELA DAVIS
civil rights leader

BENJAMIN DAVIS, SR., AND
BENJAMIN DAVIS, JR.
military leaders

SAMMY DAVIS, JR.
entertainer

FATHER DIVINE
religious leader

FREDERICK DOUGLASS
abolitionist editor

CHARLES DREW
physician

W. E. B. DU BOIS
scholar and activist

PAUL LAURENCE DUNBAR
poet

KATHERINE DUNHAM
dancer and choreographer

DUKE ELLINGTON
bandleader and composer

RALPH ELLISON
author

JULIUS ERVING
basketball great

JAMES FARMER
civil rights leader

ELLA FITZGERALD
singer

MARCUS GARVEY
black nationalist leader

JOSH GIBSON
baseball great

DIZZY GILLESPIE
musician

PRINCE HALL
social reformer

W. C. HANDY
father of the blues

WILLIAM HASTIE
educator and politician

MATTHEW HENSON
explorer

CHESTER HIMES
author

BILLIE HOLIDAY
singer

JOHN HOPE
educator

LENA HORNE
entertainer

LANGSTON HUGHES
poet

ZORA NEALE HURSTON
author

JESSE JACKSON
civil rights leader and politician

MICHAEL JACKSON
entertainer

JACK JOHNSON
heavyweight champion

JAMES WELDON JOHNSON
author

SCOTT JOPLIN
composer

BARBARA JORDAN
politician

CORETTA SCOTT KING
civil rights leader

MARTIN LUTHER KING, JR.
civil rights leader

SPIKE LEE
filmmaker

REGINALD LEWIS
entrepreneur

ALAIN LOCKE
scholar and educator

JOE LOUIS
heavyweight champion

RONALD MCNAIR
astronaut

MALCOLM X
militant black leader

THURGOOD MARSHALL
Supreme Court justice

TONI MORRISON
author

CONSTANCE BAKER
MOTLEY
*civil rights leader
and judge*

ELIJAH MUHAMMAD
religious leader

EDDIE MURPHY
entertainer

JESSE OWENS
champion athlete

SATCHEL PAIGE
baseball great

CHARLIE PARKER
musician

GORDON PARKS
photographer

ROSA PARKS
civil rights leader

SIDNEY POITIER
actor

ADAM CLAYTON
POWELL, JR.
political leader

COLIN POWELL
military leader

LEONTYNE PRICE
opera singer

A. PHILIP RANDOLPH
labor leader

PAUL ROBESON
singer and actor

JACKIE ROBINSON
baseball great

DIANA ROSS
entertainer

BILL RUSSELL
basketball great

JOHN RUSSWURM
publisher

SOJOURNER TRUTH
antislavery activist

HARRIET TUBMAN
antislavery activist

NAT TURNER
slave revolt leader

DENMARK VESEY
slave revolt leader

ALICE WALKER
author

MADAM C. J. WALKER
entrepreneur

BOOKER T. WASHINGTON
educator and racial spokesman

IDA WELLS-BARNETT
civil rights leader

WALTER WHITE
civil rights leader

OPRAH WINFREY
entertainer

STEVIE WONDER
musician

RICHARD WRIGHT
author

ON
ACHIEVEMENT

——— 🙥 ———

Coretta Scott King

Before you begin this book, I hope you will ask yourself what the word *excellence* means to you. I think that it's a question we should all ask, and keep asking as we grow older and change. Because the truest answer to it should never change. When you think of excellence, perhaps you think of success at work; or of becoming wealthy; or meeting the right person, getting married, and having a good family life.

Those important goals are worth striving for, but there is a better way to look at excellence. As Martin Luther King, Jr., said in one of his last sermons, "I want you to be first in love. I want you to be first in moral excellence. I want you to be first in generosity. If you want to be important, wonderful. If you want to be great, wonderful. But recognize that he who is greatest among you shall be your servant."

My husband, Martin Luther King, Jr., knew that the true meaning of achievement is service. When I met him, in 1952, he was already ordained as a Baptist preacher and was working toward a doctoral degree at Boston University. I was studying at the New England Conservatory and dreamed of accomplishments in music. We married a year later, and after I graduated the following year we moved to Montgomery, Alabama. We didn't know it then, but our notions of achievement were about to undergo a dramatic change.

You may have read or heard about what happened next. What began with the boycott of a local bus line grew into a national movement, and by the time he was assassinated in 1968 my husband had fashioned a black movement powerful enough to shatter forever the practice of racial segregation. What you may not have read about is where he got his method for resisting injustice without compromising his religious beliefs.

8

He adopted the strategy of nonviolence from a man of a different race, who lived in a different country, and even practiced a different religion. The man was Mahatma Gandhi, the great leader of India, who devoted his life to serving humanity in the spirit of love and nonviolence. It was in these principles that Martin discovered his method for social reform. More than anything else, those two principles were the key to his achievements.

This book is about black Americans who served society through the excellence of their achievements. It forms a part of the rich history of black men and women in America—a history of stunning accomplishments in every field of human endeavor, from literature and art to science, industry, education, diplomacy, athletics, jurisprudence, even polar exploration.

Not all of the people in this history had the same ideals, but I think you will find something that all of them had in common. Like Martin Luther King, Jr., they all decided to become "drum majors" and serve humanity. In that principle—whether it was expressed in books, inventions, or song—they found something outside themselves to use as a goal and a guide. Something that showed them a way to serve others, instead of only living for themselves.

Reading the stories of these courageous men and women not only helps us discover the principles that we will use to guide our own lives but also teaches us about our black heritage and about America itself. It is crucial for us to know the heroes and heroines of our history and to realize that the price we paid in our struggle for equality in America was dear. But we must also understand that we have gotten as far as we have partly because America's democratic system and ideals made it possible.

We are still struggling with racism and prejudice. But the great men and women in this series are a tribute to the spirit of our democratic ideals and the system in which they have flourished. And that makes their stories special and worth knowing. ❧

1

MASSACRE AT SAND CREEK

━━━━━ •❦• ━━━━━

THE HOOFBEATS ROLLED like thunder as the horses pounded along the dry bed of the stream. It was early in the morning of November 29, 1864, and to the east, far across the sand flats, a reddening low in the sky indicated that the sun was soon to come up. The riders, about 600 in all, spurred on their mounts, aware that after a nightlong journey they were finally nearing their destination, an encamp-ment of Cheyenne and Arapaho Indians along Sand Creek, a northern tributary of the Arkansas River in southeastern Colorado.

The ponies were the first to take alarm. The Cheyenne had built a corral for their horses just south of Sand Creek, and as the drumming of the hoofbeats from the south grew louder and more insistent, the penned-in animals began to mill about anxiously, whinnying and neighing. Some stamped their hooves and threw their heads into the air, as if they could sense the approaching danger.

The night had been clear and sharp, with a touch of frost and thousands of glittering stars lighting the black western sky. The stars had faded with the coming of morning, but the sun had not yet risen high enough to cast its warming rays, and the foamy sweat that appeared on the flanks of the agitated horses froze quickly in the chilly air, making the animals even more edgy.

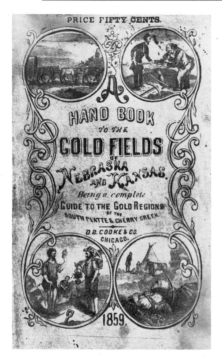

An 1859 Guide to the Gold Regions, *published a year after gold was discovered in the Front Range of the Rocky Mountains. The ensuing rush for the precious metal brought to the American West a steady stream of white settlers who competed with the local Indians for the surrounding lands.*

In the village, 600 Cheyennes and Arapahos were sleeping or just rising, rekindling cook fires or stepping through the flaps of their buffalo-skin tipis to take a first glimpse at the dawn of another day. Most of the early risers were women, awakening to prepare the morning meal. Two-thirds of the villagers, in fact, were either women or children; the majority of each tribe's men were several miles to the east, hunting buffalo.

To many of those who heard it, the incessant thunder of hoofbeats was reason for celebration, not alarm. The approaching stampede sounded as if the warriors had located a significant herd. Edmond Guerrier, the son-in-law of William Bent, a white fur trader who had built a fort along the Arkansas River 30 years earlier and had traded with and lived among the Cheyenne ever since, was among those awakened by the rumble; but he was not overly concerned. "I was sleeping in a lodge," Guerrier said later. "I heard, at first, some of the squaws outside say there were a lot of buffalo coming into camp."

The Cheyenne had reason to feel secure. They believed that just two months earlier, at Camp Weld, near the mining boomtown of Denver, Colorado, they had secured peace with Colonel John M. Chivington and the Third Colorado Cavalry.

Ever since 1858, when gold was found near Pikes Peak in the Front Range, the easternmost chain of the Rocky Mountains, settlers had been flocking to Colorado, and Pikes Peak or Bust became the motto of the thousands of pioneers who headed west to seek their fortune. Yet the notion of the West as a wide-open space just thirsting for settlers to tap its fantastic potential ignored two significant facts: There were already hundreds of Indian tribes living on the land, and they considered it to be their own.

In 1859, Little Raven, an Arapaho chief, visited Denver and wished the local whites great success in their search for the yellow metal. He also expressed the hope that they would not stay long after they found all the gold they needed. But the whites had no intention of leaving, and the Cheyenne and Arapaho in Colorado soon found themselves in the way of the white settlers.

Older and more experienced chiefs recognized that the whites had come to stay. Accordingly, the venerable Black Kettle and White Antelope of the Cheyenne, along with four other Arapaho and Cheyenne chiefs, signed a peace treaty with the whites in 1861. The terms of the treaty stated that the Cheyenne and Arapaho agreed to live within a triangular piece of territory between the Arkansas River and Sand Creek. By their own understanding, the Indians did not cede their remaining lands to the whites and retained the right to move freely about the Colorado Territory when they needed to hunt buffalo. This right was very important because the Sand Creek area was not particularly rich in game, and without the buffalo, the Indians would starve.

But peace did not come. The number of settlers in Colorado continued to grow, as did the number of violent encounters between settlers and Indians. Colorado politicians asserted that the Indians had agreed, by the terms of the 1861 treaty, to allow the construction of a railroad across their lands, a claim that the Indians vehemently denied had been part of the agreement.

Younger and more militant leaders of the Cheyenne, such as Roman Nose and the members of the warrior society known as *Hotimatanio*, or the Dog Soldiers, urged that the treaty be renounced. Meanwhile, Colorado's governor, John Evans, pressed the Cheyenne to exchange their hunting rights for a reservation, where food would be provided for them. The Indians, including White Antelope and Black Kettle, resisted.

Arapaho chief Little Raven acted as a spokesman for the Native Americans in 1859 by telling the white pioneers to leave Colorado as soon as they had mined enough gold. The settlers made it clear that they were not going to depart the territory, however, and two years later the Arapaho and Cheyenne signed a peace treaty with U.S. Army officials.

Realizing that what could not be obtained by diplomacy could be gained by force, Evans unleashed Colonel Chivington, the territorial military commander, in 1864. A bloodthirsty zealot and former Methodist minister known as the Fighting Parson, Chivington signed up miners, farmers, gold prospectors, and denizens of Denver's rollicking and rowdy saloons for 100 days of service in the Third Colorado Cavalry. These murderous volunteers began to call themselves the Hundred Dazers.

In the spring of 1864, Chivington sent his poorly trained, undisciplined forces from Denver into the surrounding territory. Their orders, according to Lieutenant George S. Eayre, one of Chivington's officers, were to "burn villages and kill Cheyennes wherever and whenever found." Black Kettle's band was attacked without provocation at a temporary encampment on Ash Creek, as was a band of Dog Soldiers just north of Denver and another Cheyenne encampment near Cedar Bluffs.

In each case, the Indians fought back, though without great success; but it was enough provocation for Evans to claim that they had gone to war. "For this the Great Father is angry," he warned the Cheyenne in an announcement issued on June 27 and addressed to the "friendly Indians of the Plains." "He will certainly hunt them out and punish them, but he does not want to injure those who remain friendly to the whites; he desires to protect and take care of them. For this purpose I direct that all friendly Indians keep away from those who are at war, and go to places of safety." Specifically, friendly Cheyenne and Arapaho were directed to return to the Sand Creek area near Fort Lyon.

Black Kettle and White Antelope were with their people at buffalo hunting camps along the Smoky Hill and Republican rivers when they received word from William Bent about Evans's directives. The

Cheyenne trusted Bent, whom they called the Little
White Man. His two wives had both been Cheyenne,
and his five children lived most of the year with their
mother's people.

"It is not my intention or wish to fight the
whites," Black Kettle had told Bent earlier that year.
"I want to be friendly and peaceable and keep my
tribe so. I am not able to fight the whites. I want to
live in peace." Bent then approached Chivington on
the Indians' behalf and inquired about the possibility
of a truce. "In reply he said he was not authorized to
make peace, and that he was then on the warpath,"
Bent recalled of his conversation with the Fighting
Parson.

Governor Evans's message convinced Black Kettle that it was worthwhile to try again for a peace,
but the chief was not sure how to go about it. A
second directive from the governor had left him
apprehensive about his people's safety should they
attempt to make their way from the Smoky Hill to
the vicinity of Fort Lyon. Evans had authorized "all
citizens of Colorado, either individually or in such
parties as they may organize, to go in pursuit of all
hostile Indians on the plains, scrupulously avoiding
all those who have responded to my call to rendezvous at the points indicated; also to kill and destroy
as enemies of the country wherever they may be
found, all such hostile Indians." In effect, Evans had
deputized the entire territory to act against the Indians, and Black Kettle feared that his band would
be attacked on its way to Sand Creek.

Acting on Bent's advice, Black Kettle dispatched
two braves, Ochinee and Eagle Head, with a message
for Major Edward J. Wynkoop, the commander at
Fort Lyon. The warriors told Wynkoop that Black
Kettle wished him and his troops to escort the
Cheyenne in safety to their reservation on Sand
Creek. Wynkoop, who was a relative newcomer to

the West, was confused. He worried that the Indians on the Smoky Hill, whom he knew far outnumbered his 100 cavalrymen, might be plotting a trap, and his suspicions were not eased by his advisers, such as Indian agent Samuel Colley, who stated that he believed "a little powder and lead" would be the best food for the Indians.

Still, in early September, Wynkoop, whom the Indians called Tall Chief, agreed to ride for Sand Creek, with Ochinee and Eagle Head serving as both guides and hostages. "At the first sign of treachery from your people," warned Tall Chief, "I will kill you."

"The Cheyennes do not break their word," Ochinee replied. "If they should do so, I would not care to live longer."

In the course of their ride and the subsequent parley with Black Kettle and White Antelope, Wynkoop would come to believe and trust the Indians. "I felt myself in the presence of superior beings," Wynkoop said later of the Cheyenne, "and these were the representatives of a race that I heretofore looked upon without exception as being cruel, treacherous, and bloodthirsty without feeling or affection for friend or kindred."

At the Smoky Hill, he was even further impressed with the sincerity of Black Kettle's expressed desire to make peace with the whites. Tall Chief explained that he had only limited power among the whites, but he promised to do all he could to prevent the soldiers from launching further attacks. He also persuaded seven Cheyenne and Arapaho chiefs to come with him to Denver and meet in a council with Colonel Chivington and Governor Evans.

After a 400-mile journey, Wynkoop's cavalry and the Indian chiefs reached Denver on September 28. The Indians rode in a flatbed wagon drawn by mules; above the wagon, a huge American flag flew proudly.

Colonel John M. Chivington, an Indian-hating former Methodist minister known as the Fighting Parson, was appointed commander of the Colorado Volunteer Cavalry's Third Regiment in the summer of 1864. The unit was supposedly formed to protect the territory's white population from attacks by unfriendly Arapaho and Cheyenne; but Beckwourth, to his great regret, soon witnessed the real reason for the mustering of Chivington's troops: to annihilate all the Native Americans in Colorado.

The Stars and Stripes had been given to Black Kettle the year before, when the chief had called upon President Abraham Lincoln in the White House during a treaty visit to the nation's capital. When in camp, Black Kettle always flew the flag above his tipi; he had been promised that no soldiers would ever fire upon his people so long as he did.

From the outset, the parley went poorly. Wynkoop was forced to use all his persuasive powers simply to convince Evans to meet with the Indians. The governor was of the opinion that there was no sense in negotiating; the Indians should be punished militarily. This was also the opinion, he informed Wynkoop, of the ranking military officer in the region, General Samuel Curtis, who had telegraphed

Chivington a chillingly clear message to that effect: "I want no peace till the Indians suffer more."

According to Evans, peace would also constitute a waste of manpower and resources. "But what shall I do with the Third Colorado Regiment if I make peace?" he asked the shocked young lieutenant. "They have been raised to kill Indians, and they must kill Indians."

Wynkoop was nonetheless able to prevail over such brusque sentiments; Evans and Chivington were persuaded to meet with the chiefs at Camp Weld. Black Kettle opened the negotiations. His message was translated from the Cheyenne by John Smith, a longtime Indian trader and friend of the Cheyenne:

> On sight of your circular of June 27, 1864, I took hold of the matter, and have now come to talk to you about it. . . . Major Wynkoop proposed that we come to see you. We have come with our eyes shut, following his handful of men, like coming through the fire. All we ask is that we may have peace with the whites. We want to hold you by the hand. You are our father. We have been traveling through a cloud. The sky has been dark ever since the war began. These braves who are with me are willing to do what I say. We want to take good tidings home to our people, so that they may sleep in peace. I want you to give all these chiefs of the soldiers here to understand that we are for peace, and that we have made peace, that we may not be mistaken by them for enemies. I have not come here with a little wolf bark, but have come to talk plain with you. We must live near the buffalo or starve. When we came we came free, without any apprehension, to see you, and when I go home and tell my people that I have taken your hand, and the hands of all the chiefs here in Denver, they will feel well.

The aging chief's dignified plea elicited only an ambiguous response. "I am not a big war chief, but all the soldiers in this country are at my command," the Fighting Parson said. "My rule of fighting white men or Indians is to fight them until they lay down their arms and submit to military authority. [The Indians] are nearer to Major Wynkoop than anyone else, and they can go to him when they are ready to do that."

Chivington's message was not very clear, but Black Kettle and White Antelope interpreted it to mean they would be left alone if they brought their people to Sand Creek. Besides, Wynkoop was still in command at Fort Lyon, and they trusted him.

"So now we broke up our camp on the Smoky Hill," remembered George Bent, the mixed-blood son of Little White Man, who was then living with the Cheyenne, "and moved down to Sand Creek, about forty miles northeast of Fort Lyon. From this new camp [we] went in and visited Major Wynkoop, and the people of the fort seemed so friendly that after a short time the Arapahoes left us and moved right down to the fort, where they went into camp and received regular rations."

But Wynkoop was not destined to remain in command at Fort Lyon for long. His intercession on behalf of the Cheyenne had angered his superiors, and in the first week of November he was replaced by Major Scott Anthony, an officer of Chivington's Colorado volunteers.

Anthony's first act as commander was to cut the rations that the Arapaho had been receiving. A couple of days later, when some unarmed Arapaho approached the fort with buffalo hides for trade, he ordered his guards to fire upon them. The Indians had "annoyed" him enough, Anthony confided to his colleagues, and "that was the only way to get rid of them."

Meanwhile, in Denver, Chivington had issued new orders to his troops: "Kill all the Indians you come across."

On November 27, Chivington himself, at the head of 600 volunteer cavalrymen, arrived at Fort Lyon with the stated intention of riding against the Indians at Sand Creek. Anthony welcomed

William Bent, a successful fur trader and longtime friend of the Cheyenne, attempted to mediate a second peace between the Native Americans and the white settlers in the late summer of 1864. He warned Cheyenne chief Black Kettle that Colonel John M. Chivington was "on the warpath" and thus convinced the Arapaho and Cheyenne it was in their best interests to broach another truce.

Cheyenne chief Black Kettle (middle row, center) and Colonel John M. Chivington (front row, right) attend a summit meeting at Camp Weld, near the mining boomtown of Denver, Colorado, on September 28, 1864. The colonel had little interest in negotiating a peace with the Indians at the conference because he was planning to launch a surprise attack on their tribes.

him, confiding that he had been eagerly "waiting for a chance to pitch into them." When three of Anthony's officers—Captain Silas Soule and Lieutenants Joseph Cranmer and James Connor—protested that an attack on Black Kettle was "murder in every sense of the word," the Fighting Parson became enraged. "Damn any man who sympathizes with the Indians," he blustered. His sense of duty was clear. "I have come to kill Indians," he explained, "and believe it is right and honorable to use any means under God's heaven to kill Indians."

At about eight o'clock on the night of November 28, under clear, cold skies, the cavalry saddled up and moved out in columns of four. At dawn's early light,

their galloping hoofbeats began to awake the slum-
bering Cheyenne encampment. George Bent was still
asleep when the sounds of unusual movement about
the camp roused him. He threw off his blankets and
rushed outside his tipi. "From down the creek," he
recalled, "a large body of soldiers was advancing at a
rapid trot....More soldiers could be seen making for
the Indian pony herds to the south of the camps; in
the camps themselves all was confusion and noise—
men, women, and children rushing out of the lodges
partly dressed; women and children screaming at the
sight of the troops; men running back into the lodges
for their arms. . . . I looked toward the chief's lodge
and saw that Black Kettle had a large American flag
tied to the end of a long lodgepole and was standing in front of his lodge, holding the pole, with the
flag fluttering in the gray light of the winter dawn.
I heard him call to the people not to be afraid, that
the soldiers would not hurt them; then the troops
opened fire from two sides of the camp."

Among those killed in the first volley were the
75-year-old White Antelope and the Arapaho chief
Left Hand. Both had approached the soldiers impas-
sively, with their arms folded, all the while counseling
their people that they had nothing to fear from the
whites, who were their friends.

After the first bloody salvo, pandemonium ensued. Black Kettle ran up the white flag of surrender
next to Old Glory, but the soldiers rode to and fro
among the Indians' lodges, firing at anything that
moved. Screams and shouts filled the air. Most of
those killed were old men and women and children;
all, including infants, were scalped, and many were
mutilated sexually. (Before the attack, Chivington
had encouraged his men to "kill and scalp all; nits
make lice.") Eyewitnesses reported "indiscriminate
slaughter of men, women, and children"; a five-year-
old girl was dragged from a hiding place in the sand

and shot through the head with a pistol; a fetus was cut from its mother's womb.

One figure moved purposefully amid the chaos and carnage. Jim Beckwourth was now 64 years of age, and an almost unimaginable profusion of wilderness experience had exhausted some of his legendary vigor; his once powerful frame, though still impressive, was somewhat stooped with rheumatism, and his eyesight was not what it had been. Long ago, Beckwourth had traded life as a slave in Missouri for the footloose, free-rambling ways of the western adventurer. He had rambled from Florida to California, across the Rocky Mountains and the Sierra Nevada, fought the Seminole and led the Crow into battle, panned for gold, hunted for furs, and guided some of the first wagon trains into California. But his trail was coming to an end.

As a black man, Beckwourth had often found himself an outcast among the predominantly white settlers of the West, and his exploits, although comparable to those of such legends as Kit Carson and Jim Bridger, had earned him only a fraction of their fame. That is, when they were credited to him at all, for in some circles Beckwourth was best known as a teller of tall tales. He was, according to some, nothing but a "gaudy liar."

At Sand Creek, the aging Beckwourth found himself in a familiar position. He was caught between a white society that at best granted him only grudging acceptance and in which he was only fitfully at ease and often adrift; and the world of the Indians, where he had known some of his greatest happiness yet also felt as if he was an outsider. Beckwourth had at one time been one of the greatest war chiefs of the Crow nation; in his day, he had also been, according to one historian, "the greatest Indian fighter of his generation."

"Our new Indian policy—Which is the savage?" asks a 19th-century political cartoon inspired by the U.S. Army's brutal attacks on Native Americans. Beckwourth might have asked the same question: Coerced into serving as an interpreter and guide for the Colorado Volunteer Cavalry's Third Regiment, he was a witness to the wholesale slaughter of Arapaho and Cheyenne at Sand Creek, in southeastern Colorado, on November 29, 1864. He subsequently appeared before a military commission to testify about the army's inhumane actions during the massacre.

Now in restless semiretirement with the most recent of his countless wives, Beckwourth had been dragged unwillingly from his Denver home by Chivington and ordered, at the threat of hanging for noncompliance, to guide the cavalry to the slaughter. As a trader, he had spent much time during the previous 14 years with these particular bands of the Cheyenne and the Arapaho. They knew him as Medicine Calf, and he considered them his friends.

As the cavalry entered the camp, Beckwourth rode at Chivington's right hand, from where he witnessed White Antelope "running out to meet the command at the time the battle had commenced, holding up his hands and saying 'Stop! Stop!' He spoke it in as plain English as I can. He stopped and folded his arms until shot down."

With the massacre raging around him, Beckwourth moved purposefully from lodge to lodge until he found the person he was looking for: Charlie Bent, another son of William Bent, his old friend and colleague in the fur trade. Beckwourth guided the young man to a wagon being used as an ambulance and hid him among some wounded soldiers until he could turn Charlie over to his brother Robert, who, like Beckwourth, had been forced by Chivington to ride against the Cheyenne.

By nightfall, the shooting had ended. The weather had turned brutally cold, and the corpses strewn about the village at Sand Creek began to freeze. "I did not see a body of man, woman, or child but was scalped, and in many instances their bodies were mutilated in the most horrible manner," Lieutenant Connor later testified.

Drunkenness and inexperience had hindered the volunteers in the performance of their gruesome duty and mercifully allowed many of the Indians, including Black Kettle, to escape. The survivors tramped some 50 miles through a lightly falling snow to rejoin the warriors in their hunting camp on the Smoky Hill. The reunion, according to George Bent, was a "terrible scene. Everyone was crying, even the warriors, and the women and children screaming and wailing. Nearly everyone present had lost some relatives or friends, and many of them in their grief were gashing themselves with their knives until the blood flowed in streams."

Back at Colonel Chivington's camp on the battlefield at Sand Creek, there was one more death to be tallied. Among the captives was the interpreter John Smith's mixed-blood son, Jack, who had been living with the Cheyenne and was reputed to have

led a militant band that had raided several settlements. As Beckwourth sat in a tent with the captives,
a shot was fired from outside through the open flap;
it shattered Smith's chest. Beckwourth sprang to his
feet and raced outside, where he met a soldier with a
gun in his hand.

"I am afraid the damn son of a bitch is not dead,
and I will finish him," the soldier said.

Horrified by all that he had seen that day, Beckwourth grabbed the man by the arm. "Let him go to
rest," he said. "He is dead." ✤

2

THE HOWLING
WILDERNESS
◆❦◆

THE WINNING OF the West is America's great historical epic. "The West is the great word of our history," wrote Woodrow Wilson, scholar and 28th president of the United States. There have been no more enduring symbols of America than the cowboy and the Indian, just as there is no denying the hold they retain on the American imagination.

The images are indelible, formed by countless novels, explorers' journals, historical accounts, paintings, and movies: Bystanders scurry as a dusty street empties and two gunfighters face off under the blazing sun at high noon; artfully concealed on a high bluff, a band of Indian warriors watches silently as, far below them, a keelboat carries fur traders upriver; a trumpet sounds, and the cavalry thunders down into an Indian village, swords drawn and rifles blazing. The stories have been told so many times that they have taken on a reality quite separate from their historical truth. They now shimmer with the aura of myth and legend.

There is something missing, however. In the West, as the story has been presented, men and women, colored white and red, fought, trusted, tricked, loved, hated, and killed each other while struggling to possess a region of unparalleled physical beauty and overwhelming natural abundance. But blacks, too, played roles in this monumental American drama.

A "howling wilderness" was how Beckwourth described the American frontier. The rough and tumble region lured his father, Jennings Beckwith, from the East Coast, then cast its spell over Beckwourth, too.

27

Blacks were among the fur trappers who blazed the trails across the plains and mountains that generations of pioneers would use as they made their way west. They left behind the constraints of the white man's civilization for the more congenial way of life of the Plains Indians and attained positions of honor and respect within their adopted tribes. They rode with the cavalry against the Indians in its mission to clear the West for American civilization. They founded permanent settlements. They searched for gold and silver in the hope of striking it rich. They hunted the buffalo. They fought the Spanish for possession of the Southwest. They stole horses and rigged card games. They were entrusted by generals and governors to deliver messages and the mail. They led wagon trains from the murderous sands of the Great Basin across the snowcapped mountains to safety in verdant California. Some, like Jim Beckwourth, did all these things. And some, like Jim Beckwourth, told of all they had done.

James Pierson Beckwourth "was born in Fredericksburg, Virginia, on the 26th of April, 1798," according to the first sentence of his autobiography, *The Life and Adventures of James P. Beckwourth, Mountaineer, Scout, Pioneer, and Chief of the Crow Nation*, which was published in 1856 and penned from his spoken recollections by a dissolute former temperance crusader named T. D. Bonner. Subsequent historical research has shown that on the matter of the date and place of Beckwourth's entrance into the world, as on many other issues, the veracity of his memory is open to question.

Unfortunately, in many cases the historical record is not much clearer. There are few documents with which to trace Beckwourth's days in the untamed West; much of what is known about his life has been derived from reminiscences, deduction, and a not inconsiderable amount of speculation. One can be

VIEW OF FREDERICKSBURG, VA.

sure that he played a prominent role in the opening of the West, but the details of his actions and the words he uttered have been lost forever.

On the matter of his birth, Beckwourth no doubt spoke what he believed to be true. No written documentation of his birth appears to exist, if it ever did, so he probably told Bonner what he recalled having been told himself. In the freewheeling West, where a man could invent his own reality, such details were of minimal importance. Even the name by which he is known to history, and which graced the title of his life story, is only an approximation of his actual identity.

In all likelihood, Beckwourth was born in 1800. His father's name was Jennings Beckwith, not Beckwourth, and he came from a prominent Virginia landholding family that traced its ancestry to a knight who fought with the Norman king William the Conqueror at the Battle of Hastings in 1066. Jen-

Beckwourth claimed to have spent his early years in Fredericksburg, a river town in northeast Virginia. He moved with his father to the eastern Missouri wilderness in 1808.

One of the first white Americans to cross the Appalachians, Daniel Boone saw thousands of pioneers follow his footsteps west after he blazed a trail across the mountains into Kentucky. He settled there first, then moved to eastern Missouri and lived near the Point, where Beckwourth spent the latter part of his childhood.

nings was regarded as something of a black sheep by his family, possibly because of his relationship with Beckwourth's mother. Her lineage, as well as her name, character, and station in life, is unknown. But it is virtually certain that she was a slave on the Beckwith plantation, which was located in Frederick County, not Fredericksburg, and was, according to a number of sources, a light-skinned black woman of mixed blood.

Jim's mother, it is believed, had a longstanding relationship with Jennings Beckwith that was based on mutual affection, and they lived more or less openly as man and wife after his legal spouse died and he moved to Missouri in 1808. This open liaison would have been considered a transgression of social mores by white Virginia society. But by relocating in Missouri, Jennings was able to reject the genteel life of a plantation owner in favor of the rough-hewn way of the frontier.

Moving west placed Jennings Beckwith at the forefront of the stream of American settlers who crossed the Mississippi River to Missouri during the first two decades of the 19th century. Many of these pioneers came from Tennessee or Kentucky, where they had settled after crossing the Appalachian Mountains from the Atlantic seaboard. Among these settlers was the legendary pathfinder Daniel Boone.

During the American Revolution—several decades before Jennings Beckwith had moved to Missouri—Boone blazed a trail across the mountains, the famed Wilderness Road, that enabled thousands of pioneers to follow his footsteps west. Boone thus became the first white man in America to bring his family to Kentucky, and Boonesborough, where he and his family settled, became the westernmost extension of the American frontier. By 1799, however, Boone claimed that sparsely settled Kentucky had grown too crowded, and he moved his family to

Missouri, where for a time he was able to fulfill his lifelong dream of owning his own land in a region rich in game.

Boone was the prototype of the first generation of American westering explorer, moving the country's civilization from the coast to the interior, as far west as the Mississippi. Jim Beckwourth was a representative of the next generation, whose restlessness led them all the way to the Pacific, extending the United States's dominion from "sea to shining sea."

Jim's restlessness was in part an inheritance from his father. Jennings Beckwith shared with Boone a temperament that made him far more at home in the wilderness, tending traps along a riverbank or hunting deer in a pine thicket, than in more settled pursuits, such as business or agriculture. The 1,280 heavily wooded acres he owned between the Mississippi and Missouri rivers, in a section called the Point (not far from the settlement and present-day city of St. Charles), were used by him essentially as a hunting and fishing park; he was at best indifferent to the notion of making his land profitable through farming, and several different portions of his property had to be auctioned because of his failure to pay taxes.

Having come to Missouri in search of solitude and freedom, Jennings Beckwith took no part in the political or social life of St. Charles or nearby St. Louis. His love of the wild and proficiency in woodcraft became so well known that upon his death in 1835 an obituary likened him to Leatherstocking, as Natty Bumppo, the rifleman hero of James Fenimore Cooper's enormously popular novels of frontier life, was known. (Many historians believe that Cooper actually based his character on Boone.) According to that same obituary, "much" of Jennings Beckwith's life was spent "wandering in the *Far West* on hunting excursions with the Indians and of late years he would live with men [who] would fish with him in summer or fox hunt in winter." As "he had insuperable objections to spending time profitably . . . he lived poor but respectable and esteemed by many friends."

Though legally a slave, Jim was never treated as one by his father, with whom, by the only evidence that exists, he enjoyed a loving relationship. He came and went as he pleased, and at the age of 10 he was sent to school in St. Louis rather than ordered to work in the fields. There he learned to read and write with a greater degree of proficiency than many of his contemporaries on the frontier could boast, and if Bonner's transcription of his speech is accurate, in later life Jim possessed a facility of language, characterized by a keen power of description, that sometimes bordered on the eloquent. Some of those who met Jim in later years observed that he spoke much better than did most of his fellow mountain men.

When not in the classroom, Jim spent much of his time traipsing with his father through the thick stands of ash, cottonwood, hickory, elder, elm, and hackberry trees that covered the Beckwith land, hunting deer, wild turkey, possum, quail, squirrel, and even the occasional bear, receiving a kind of outdoors apprenticeship that would serve him well in later life. The Point was still at that time, in Beckwourth's words, very much a "howling wilderness," as was the surrounding territory. Fewer than 10,000 non-Indians occupied the almost 70,000 square miles that in 1821 would become the state of Missouri, and well more than half of these people lived in St. Louis, the boisterous boomtown at the confluence of the Mississippi and Missouri rivers.

Because it marked the westernmost edge of the American frontier, Missouri attracted all sorts of adventurers. St. Louis became the jumping-off point for exploratory and entrepreneurial expeditions into the continent's interior. Fur traders plied the

territory's rivers, seeking Indians with whom to exchange iron and metal goods—sewing needles, guns,
ammunition, copper kettles, axes—for beaver skins.
Around St. Louis, along or near the Mississippi and
the Missouri, a handful of hardy individuals engaged
in the backbreaking work of clearing the land and
planting crops. Others, like Jennings Beckwith and
Daniel Boone, indulged their love for a life lived
out-of-doors and far removed from civilization's
restraints.

The Indians' reaction to the white man's incursion varied from tribe to tribe. The Sac and
Fox, Kickapoo, Potawatomi, Osage, and others had
been dealing with fur traders since such intrepid
Frenchman as the Sieur de LaSalle first ventured
down the Mississippi in the latter part of the 17th
century, and the economies of these tribes had grown
quite dependent on trade goods. Through the early
1800s, fur traders relied on the Indians to do the
actual trapping and preparation of pelts and skins.
The traders either ventured to the various Indian
villages or established fortified trading posts to which
the Indians brought their pelts. Rampant competi-
tion among white traders gave the Indians a considerable degree of choice as to whom they would sell
their pelts.

Mutual interests ensured that more-or-less har-
monious relations prevailed between the traders and
the Indians. The traders needed the Indians to per-
form the actual work of fur trapping and preparation,
so the last thing they wanted to do was drive them
from the land. The Indians wanted the goods that
the white men brought, which included woven cloth,
wool blankets, glass beads, and alcohol, so they were
willing to allow the traders to come into their territory.

The Indians did not feel as benevolent toward
settlers. (For that matter, neither did most fur traders;

Fur traders beat a hasty retreat from a group of attacking Indians. An increasing number of Native Americans objected to having their territory invaded by whites as the 18th century wore on, although many tribes had been dealing peacefully with fur traders since the late 17th century.

because it displaced both Indians and game, settlement was generally bad for business.) During the early stages of the fur trade's existence, the Indians were in control of their land. But as soon as white settlers began to establish farms and towns on Indian territories, it meant a transfer in legal and actual land ownership and control.

By the time of Beckwourth's childhood, Indian raids on American settlements were not uncommon in Missouri. In later years, he remembered that the owners of nearby tracts would join together to build a stockade to which they and their families could repair when the Indians were on the warpath. Work in the fields was usually done in shifts, with those off duty acting as lookouts for the other laborers.

The situation worsened after the outbreak of the War of 1812, which the United States and Great Britain fought in part over control of the territory west of the Appalachians. In Missouri, as elsewhere on the frontier, the Indians' desire to drive off the American settlers merged with Britain's desire to win undisputed control of the West. Armed and encouraged by their British allies, the Indians around the Point, which was too remote to be effectively protected by the U.S. Army in those youthful days of the fast-growing republic, grew so aggressive that the settlers were forced to form their own militia.

One of the militia's commanding officers was Nathan Boone, son of the aging pioneer. The indefatigable Daniel, then 78 years old, was bitterly disappointed at having his application for active military service rejected by the army. Nevertheless, he participated in several of the militia's operations.

Jim was too young to take part in such action, but later on he recalled the day when a war party of 155 canoes appeared at Portage de Sioux, about two miles from his father's house. The Indians, he said, intended to "cut off all the white inhabitants of the surrounding country." The militia soon arrived, a bloody battle ensued, and the Indians, having incurred "great loss," withdrew.

Although the same force regrouped to menace St. Louis soon afterward, the city's cannon proved too formidable for them, and the Indians subsequently limited themselves to guerrilla-style raids on isolated settlers. Many of Jennings Beckwith's neighbors had their cabins and crops burned and their horses and other animals stolen. Some of the settlers were even less fortunate. To the end of his life, Jim remembered the horror and fear he felt at discovering the mutilated corpses of two of his playmates not far from the charred ruin that had once been their home.

Following the war's end in 1815, hostilities between the whites and the settlers near St. Charles lessened, with the Indians resigning themselves to the already-existing American presence and concentrating their efforts on preventing further encroachment. Nevertheless, the tumultuous events had given Jim Beckwourth, he later wrote, the "rudiments" of his "knowledge of the Indian character," which would prove to be of "such inestimable value . . . in [his] subsequent adventures among them." But before

these escapades took place, he set out in an altogether different direction.

In 1819 or thereabouts, Beckwourth apprenticed to George Casner and John Sutton, partners in a St. Louis blacksmith firm. The partners did not much like each other, and Beckwourth did not much like them—especially Casner—or his prospective trade. Young, restless, and striking looking if not quite handsome, Beckwourth was away from the seclusion of the Point and on his own for the first time in the big city. St. Louis was then one of the most cosmopolitan places on the continent, and he found himself much more interested in the town's glittering nightlife and its numerous attractive young women than his anvil and forge. As his nights grew longer, Beckwourth's attention to his work lessened—a state of affairs that Casner was unwilling to tolerate. Frequent arguments were the result.

Feeling himself already "quite a man" and finding the "company [he] spent time with so irresist-
ibly attractive that [he] could not bring himself
to obedience to orders," Beckwourth simply defied
Casner's requests that he alter his behavior. A final
dispute grew so heated that a passing constable was
forced to intervene. Because Beckwourth was an
apprentice and a slave, he possessed few legal rights.
Fearful that the constable would mediate in Casner's
favor, he knocked him cold and made his escape.

After three days in hiding, Beckwourth returned
to his father. Recognizing in his son the same untamed spirit that had driven him west, Jennings
Beckwith placated Casner and went to court to
arrange for his son's formal release from slavery.
Never again would Jim Beckwourth be in legal thrall
to any man; never again would he practice a trade;
never again would he make his home in the big city.
Now legally free, he would choose for himself the
most independent existence imaginable for any individual: the life of a mountain man.

3

THE FREE TRAPPER

O N FEBRUARY 13, 1822, an intriguing advertisement appeared in the *Missouri Gazette*. It read: "TO Enterprising Young Men: The Subscriber wishes to engage ONE HUNDRED MEN, to ascend the river Missouri to its source, there to be employed for one, two or three years.—For particulars, enquire of Major Andrew Henry, near the Lead Mines, in the County of Washington, (who will ascend with, and command the party) or to the subscriber at St. Louis. William H. Ashley." In all likelihood, these 64 not especially informative words constituted the most influential classified ad in the history of the United States.

Ashley was a Virginian come west to seek fame and fortune. Henry was a veteran fur trader who, in 1810 as a member of Manuel Lisa's Missouri Fur Company, had been one of the first American mountain men to follow the Missouri into the Rockies in search of beaver skins. The age of the mountain men had begun 16 years prior to Ashley's solicitation, with the return of the explorers Meriwether Lewis and William Clark from their expedition up the Missouri River from St. Louis to its source in the Rocky Mountains and beyond, all the way to the Pacific Ocean. Among the many wonders Lewis and Clark

Always eager for adventure, Beckwourth joined an 1822 expedition to Fever River in Illinois, then traveled by steamboat to New Orleans before returning to the Point, his family's home in Missouri. By that time, he said later, he was "possessed of a strong desire to see the celebrated Rocky Mountains, and the great Western wilderness so much talked about."

The 1822 advertisement for a fur-trapping expedition, headed by William Ashley and Major Andrew Henry, "to ascend the river Missouri to its source." In all likelihood, Beckwourth saw this notice in a Missouri newspaper and was a member of Ashley's party when it left St. Louis on March 10, 1823.

TO

Enterprising Young Men.

THE subscriber wishes to engage ONE HUN-DRED MEN, to ascend the river Missouri to its source, there to be employed for one, two or three years.—For particulars, enquire of Major Andrew Henry, near the Lead Mines, in the County of Washington, (who will ascend with, and command the party) or to the subscriber at St. Louis.

Wm. H. Ashley.

February 13　　——98 tf

had to report from their voyage—to that date the most comprehensive exploration of the West—was the richness of the country surrounding the Missouri in fur-bearing animals, particularly the beaver. (Felt derived from its fur was used in Europe to fashion the broad variety of beaver hats that formed an indispensable part of every gentleman's wardrobe, and several New World fortunes were made from the Old World's demand for beaver skins.)

On its return journey, the Corps of Discovery, as Lewis and Clark's party was known, encountered a couple of fur traders, Joseph Dickson and Forest Hancock, on their way upriver. Few whites ventured very far up the Missouri from St. Louis, but when Hancock and Dickson heard what Lewis and Clark had to say about the profusion of wildlife upriver, they begged the explorers to lend them a man who could guide them to the Rockies. The rugged John Colter volunteered to return to the magnificent country he had just left behind, and the three men headed upriver. Before long, numerous companies, all of them working out of St. Louis, had formed for the purpose of gathering furs from the wilderness.

These forays up the Missouri were short lived, however, due to the outbreak of the War of 1812 and the resistance of the Indian tribes that lived along the river. Still, Henry, who had made several voyages upriver and established the first American trading post west of the Continental Divide, had seen enough to be convinced that there was a fortune in furs to be trapped in the Rockies. He often said as much to his close friend and fellow officer in the Missouri militia William Ashley.

Ashley had already demonstrated considerable drive and an aptitude for moneymaking. During the War of 1812, he had made a killing by establishing a works near Potosi, Missouri, that produced saltpeter (also known as potassium nitrate), a colorless crystalline compound used in the making of gunpowder. After the war, as settlers continued to flock to Missouri, he made a tidy profit in real estate. In 1822, he was elected the new state's first lieutenant governor. But Ashley's ambition would not let him rest. He aspired to even greater wealth and political power, and in St. Louis in the 1820s the means to both was the fur trade. Together, Ashley and Henry decided to try to reopen the route to the Rockies.

Among the enterprising young men who responded to Ashley's advertisement was a veritable future hall of fame of mountain men: Jedediah Smith, a soft-spoken, Bible-toting young man who would become by most accounts the greatest of the mountain men; James Clyman, Smith's great friend, whose journal of his years in the mountains would provide a more reliable, if less exciting, counterpart to Beckwourth's account; Thomas ("Broken Hand") Fitzpatrick, a native of County Cavan in Ireland, whose hair would turn snowy white following an epic three-day battle with Indians in the Wind River Mountains; William Sublette, the future discoverer of the geysers at Yellowstone and Ashley's business successor; Jim ("Gabe") Bridger, the future discoverer of the Great Salt Lake and like Beckwourth an accomplished spinner of yarns; "Old" Hugh Glass, celebrated even among his rugged companions for his legendary toughness; Edward Rose, former Mississippi River pirate and thief, like Beckwourth a black man who would become a war chief of the Crow Indians; and Jim Beckwourth himself, hot-tempered former apprentice and slave.

Although these and many other adventurers would distinguish themselves in the mountains for many years, at the time most were comparative newcomers with little experience in the fur trade. They were suited for their new positions primarily by a love of the outdoors and a willingness for adventure. (Clyman, for example, was a land surveyor; Sublette was a constable in St. Charles; and Bridger was an apprentice blacksmith.) Not one of them had a real idea of what these adventures would entail.

Among the "particulars" they learned from Ashley and Henry was that their employers intended to take a completely new approach to the fur trade. Traditionally, fur-trading companies paid their employees a salary, generally between $200 and $400 a year, in exchange for their services. For that sum, the employees were expected to function as *traders* rather than *trappers*. They were expected to venture into a designated area, establish their presence and a headquarters—generally through the construction of a fort/trading post—and initiate friendly relations with the local Indian tribes for the purpose of inducing them to trap and hunt fur-bearing animals and bring their pelts for trade at the fort. Beaver skins were the most desirable, but depending on their location, traders also welcomed the hides of bears, foxes, otters, muskrats, martens, minks, lynxes, wolverines, wolves, elks, deer, buffalo, antelope, and weasels.

The forts served as a storehouse for both furs and the trade goods with which the company supplied

its employees for exchange with the Indians. At regular intervals—usually once every summer—the fort would be resupplied and the furs taken to the company warehouses in St. Louis for shipment east or to Europe.

Ashley and Henry proposed to change this system by making their enterprising young men into "free trappers," which meant that Beckwourth and his colleagues were expected to go into the wilderness and do the actual trapping of game themselves. Instead of a salary, they would be provided with transportation west and equipment in exchange for one half of their year's catch. The other half was their own to dispose with as they pleased, either by sale to Ashley and Henry or to a rival company.

Traders were generally bound to a fort. Free trappers, on the other hand, were welcome, even encouraged, to ramble as far as the spirit took them, so long as they returned at a set time to an arranged location—initially a fort Henry was to establish at the

For William Ashley, Major Andrew Henry, and their enterprising young men, the Rocky Mountains were the promised land, a trapper's paradise where an unimaginable abundance of beavers and other fur-bearing animals could be found.

Great Falls of the Missouri River—to sell their furs and resupply themselves.

The difficulties attached to establishing this new system became apparent right away. In the spring of 1822, Henry took a small advance force upriver to gain a foothold in the mountains. But when one of his keelboats was wrecked and sunk, resulting in the loss of $10,000 worth of trade goods, and his horses were run off and stolen by Assiniboin warriors, he had to build his fort at the confluence of the Yellowstone and Missouri rivers rather than at the Great Falls. That winter, four of his men were ambushed and killed by the Blackfoot, who had nurtured their hatred toward traders and trappers ever since a murderous encounter with Meriwether Lewis on the return leg of his journey in 1806.

An undeterred Ashley, with two keelboats and 70 of the enterprising young men, possibly including Beckwourth, set out from St. Louis on March 10, 1823, to join his partner. Not far up the Missouri, Ashley met Jedediah Smith, who had been sent by Henry with the message that he was in desperate need of more horses, which could best be obtained in trade from the Arikara Indian villages in what is now northern South Dakota. What neither Ashley, Henry, nor Smith knew was that the Arikara were not feeling particularly well disposed toward fur traders. The Arikara's great enemies were the Sioux, and traders doing business with the latter tribe had recently protected Sioux warriors from an Arikara war party. The offending traders were not members of Ashley and Henry's group, but the 600 warriors at the Arikara villages were in no mood to make distinctions.

Ashley and his men reached the Arikara villages on May 30. Despite a considerable amount of tension between the two parties, the initial parley went well, and the would-be trappers were able to obtain 19 horses. Near the end of the first day's bargaining, a fierce storm blew up, making it necessary for a shore party of several dozen men, commanded by Smith, to sleep on the beach outside the fortified walls of the villages. Ashley, meanwhile, remained with his keelboats, which he had prudently kept anchored in mid-river, out of the reach of the bands of sullen warriors who materialized from time to time during the day.

That night, around midnight, a shaken Edward Rose emerged at top speed from the Arikara villages, shouting that Aaron Stephens had been murdered. The two men had entered the village for an undisclosed purpose—most likely in search of female companionship—but only Rose had come out. Ashley told his boatmen, most of whom were French-Canadian voyageurs, to bring their skiffs to the shore and remove Smith, his men, and the horses. But Ashley's orders only added to the growing confusion. Some of the voyageurs were simply too frightened to respond; those who did found Smith and the men on the bank, infuriated by reports that Stephens had been beheaded and had his eyes gouged out, vowing revenge and refusing to move.

Daybreak brought with it a succession of shots from the Arikara villages, which forced the men on the beach to seek cover behind their newly acquired horses. (The Arikara were well armed with rifles sold to them by traders from the Hudson's Bay Company, a British concern working southward out of Canada. The Hudson's Bay Company was extremely interested in expanding its operations into the Rockies and along the upper Missouri and the Columbia River, and any belligerence displayed toward the Americans by the Indians along the Missouri served the company's interests by slowing the advance of its rivals.) The fighting lasted just 15 minutes before the traders beat a panicky retreat. In that time, 12 of them were killed, 2 were fatally wounded and died later, and 9 more suffered wounds of varying degrees of seriousness. Together, the casualties totaled one-third of Ashley's force.

It was a stunning baptism by fire for the would-be free trappers. The reaction of James Clyman was perhaps typical. "Before meeting with this defeat, I think few men had Stronger Ideas of their bravery and disregard of fear than I had," Clyman wrote, "but standing on a b[are] and open sand barr to be shot at from bihind a picketed Indian village was more than I had cont[r]acted for and some what cooled my courage." In the confusion of the retreat, Clyman "concluded to take to the open Prairie and run for life." Pursued by several Arikara warriors, he dashed for several miles before catching sight of Ashley's boats, which were heading downriver, and swam to safety.

The defeat forced Ashley to make a reassessment similar to Clyman's. It was essential that Ashley get his men to the mountains before the onset of winter, which was prime trapping season. Yet the army had been dispatched to punish the Arikara, and the outbreak of hostilities meant that the Missouri, the acknowledged route to the mountains, was effectively closed to traders.

Ashley regrouped his band and stationed it at Fort Kiowa, an outpost at the confluence of the White River and the Missouri. They were joined there by Henry and his small force. Henry had returned downriver in response to a summons brought by the stalwart Smith, whose legendary reputation for courage and hardiness began with his stand on the beach outside the Arikara villages.

In September, two groups set out from Fort Kiowa. Henry, with 13 men, was bound for his post at the mouth of the Yellowstone. Smith, with somewhere between 11 and 16 companions, including Sublette, Rose, and Clyman, was directed to find an overland route across the Rockies and to take his men to the beaver-rich Columbia River territory. Meanwhile, Ashley would return to St. Louis, attempt to scrounge provisions—his capital was running low—with which to resupply his men in the spring, and launch his ultimately unsuccessful campaign for governor of Missouri.

Smith took his small band due west across the plains of South Dakota, through country so arid that men and horses collapsed from thirst. The tiny caravan passed through the desolate Badlands, which an unimpressed Clyman described as a "pile of ashes," and the Black Hills, an outlying range of the Rockies, which Smith and his men were in all likelihood the first white men to see.

Near the end of their crossing, they surprised a grizzly bear near its lair. In Clyman's words, the fearsome beast "did not hesitate a moment but sprang on the captain." The bear having taken "nearly all his head in his capacious mouth," Smith was left with several broken ribs, a ruined ear, and a good portion of his scalp torn off. Clyman stitched the wounds as best he could, and in 10 days, remarkably, Smith was ready to continue on.

Over the course of several wintry months, Smith led his men, trapping as they went, across the Thunder Basin region of northeastern Wyoming to the Powder River, then across the Bighorn Mountains to the Bighorn River basin, which he described as "beautiful, fit for cultivation, and filled with game." From the Bighorn, they moved northwest across the Owl Creek Mountains into the stunning valley of the Wind River, where they met the remnants of Henry's Yellowstone party.

Discouraged by Blackfoot pillagings and continued hardship, Henry had decided that Ashley's scheme was unworkable and was about to abandon

John Wesley Powell, the greatest post–Civil War explorer of the American West, was the first white man to navigate the length of the Green and Colorado rivers, including the rapids of the Grand Canyon. During his expedition, he discovered evidence of William Ashley's voyage along the gorges of the Green River in 1825.

the fur trade. But some of his men were not yet ready to give up. The new party spent the winter at a Crow Indian encampment before pushing on.

In February, Smith moved northward and attempted to cross the Rockies through Union Pass, but icy blizzards prevented his passing. Learning from the Crow of "easier" country farther south, he took his men in that direction, until they reached the Sweetwater River, which he then followed west to a 20-mile-wide, easily traversed stretch of grassy rolling hills that separated the Wind River Mountains from an equally rugged range farther south. This was the legendary South Pass, which in years to come would serve as the passage through the Rockies for hundreds of thousands of pioneers bound for California and Oregon.

Smith wasted no time pondering the ramifications of his discovery, for the Crow had told him that on the far side of the mountains beavers were so numerous that one did not even need traps to capture them; one could simply walk among them with a club and conk them on the head. Beyond the pass, at the headwaters of the Green River, the delighted trappers found this information to be only scarcely an exaggeration, and they split into several small groups, wandering far afield in search of pelts. In the process, they added immeasurably to the store of knowledge regarding the geography of the West.

In November 1824, Ashley at last set out from Fort Atkinson, at the junction of the Missouri and the Platte rivers. In the interim, Henry had returned downriver, bringing with him his determination to quit the fur trade and a cache of skins that earned Ashley enough money to outfit his expedition and buy supplies for the men in the mountains. Clyman and Fitzpatrick had also returned, bearing news of the adventures of Smith and the others and of the richness of the mountain streams.

Though Ashley agreed with Henry that it was too difficult and costly to hold and maintain trading posts, he now had a new idea. Guided by Clyman and Fitzpatrick, he would attempt to track down all his parties in the mountains and bring their supplies directly to them.

At the head of 80 men traveling in the dead of winter, Ashley took five months to reach the Green River, from where he sent three parties north, west, and south in search of his widely dispersed enterprising young men. When found, his free trappers were to be instructed to rendezvous at the end of June 1825 at Henry's Fork, further down the Green, near where it connects with the Yampa River. Ashley, with a few men, then voyaged downriver through the Green's stupendous gorges in a couple of bull boats, circular craft made by stretching buffalo hides over a wooden framework.

Though Ashley almost drowned several times in the rapids for which the river has become famous, his voyage was a landmark in the history of exploration. Nearly 50 years later, the geologist John Wesley Powell, in becoming the first man to navigate the Green and the Colorado rivers downstream all the way through the Grand Canyon, was astonished to find evidence of Ashley's voyage. Before Powell, it had been assumed that no one had been audacious enough to challenge the swirling waters and steep canyons of the Green.

Ashley was displaying equal confidence in expecting that his search parties would be successful in rounding up his trappers, for his men were spread out over literally thousands of square miles. Nevertheless, at the end of June, 120 American trappers—all of Henry's men plus employees of other American companies at work in the mountains—converged on Henry's Fork, where for several glorious days they talked, renewed old friendships, began new ones,

Native Americans cross the Missouri River in bull boats, circular vessels featuring buffalo hides stretched over a wooden framework. William Ashley made use of such crafts during his 1825 voyage along the Green River.

drank, caroused, sold furs, and resupplied themselves for another year in the mountains.

Thus was born one of the most storied traditions of the Old West: the annual rendezvous of the fur trappers. For the next 15 years—the heyday of the fur trade in the West—the rendezvous was held each summer at a prearranged spot in the Rockies. These gatherings were the business meetings of the fur trade. At the rendezvous, free trappers would exchange and sell their year's catch and obtain the supplies they needed to spend another year in the mountains, while the representatives of the various trading companies assembled to collect or purchase furs and sell the trappers their supplies. The rendezvous was also a riotous celebration, as the trappers unleashed the pent-up energies of a year's worth of solitude and isolation in every manner of raucous excess.

Ashley's improvised solution to the problem of maintaining trading posts so far removed from St. Louis proved a brilliant success. As his enterprising young men headed back into the mountains at the close of the 1825 rendezvous, he made his way back to St. Louis with more than $50,000 worth of furs. His take the next year was even more lucrative, enabling him to sell his interest in the company to Smith and Sublette and devote his attention to politics.

To the frustration of historians and biographers, Beckwourth's precise role in these adventures has proved impossible to determine. Historians are still piecing together the geographical details of the travels of the men of the Rocky Mountain Fur Company, as Ashley's company was known in its incarnation under Smith and Sublette. Collectively, the enterprising young men, by now hardened outdoorsman, wandered virtually the entire West—from the Mississippi to the Pacific, from the Missouri to the Rio Grande, from Oregon to New Mexico—in their years in the wilderness, and there is no reason to believe that Beckwourth was any less active. Unfortunately, few kept any records of their travels.

As for Beckwourth, his autobiography is more distinguished as entertainment than historical record. His account of these years, while quite exciting, is impossibly contradictory. It places him at the center of events known to have occurred simultaneously several hundred miles apart, includes as his own adventures episodes known to have befallen others, and is hopelessly confused as to dates and chronology.

Even a detail as elementary as when Beckwourth decided that he was one of the stalwart young fellows that Ashley was looking for has proven elusive. Following his altercation with the constable at Casner's blacksmith shop, he apparently spent some time back home with his father—perhaps as long as several years—before accompanying an expedition on a voyage of nine days up the Mississippi River from St. Louis to the site of present-day Galena, Illinois, where a settlement was being founded near some recently established lead mines.

By the only account available—his own—Beckwourth seems not to have done too much mining. Instead, while the other settlers were busy organizing themselves in "companies" for protection against the Indians, he spent most of his time hunting. "The Indians soon became very friendly to me," he recalled later, "and I soon grew indebted to them for showing me their choicest hunting grounds."

Perhaps it was at Fever River, as Galena was then known, that Beckwourth read or heard about Ashley's advertisement, but there is simply no way of knowing. Some historians place Beckwourth with Ashley, Smith, and the rest at the critical battle at the Arikara villages. Yet Beckwourth himself makes no mention of his participation and says that at the time he was riding west with Ashley along the Kansas River—a clear impossibility.

Ashley, but not Beckwourth, says that Beckwourth was among the party that left Fort Atkinson in November 1824, and several episodes in Beckwourth's account seem to accord with events that occurred on Ashley's way west. But few of Beckwourth's contemporaries, and few historians since, credit his claims that he was the first member of Ashley's party to lay eyes on the Green or that he was the one who personally saved Ashley from drowning in the river's rapids. Beckwourth's tale of his heroics in singlehandedly plucking Ashley from the "suck" of the Setskedee, as the Green was then known, has become perhaps the best-known episode of his book. But as Beckwourth himself was the first one to point out, he had, by the time his employer's bull boats were being swamped, long since been assigned to Clyman's party, which was some 150 miles away from the scene of Ashley's near disaster.

No portion of Beckwourth's autobiography has earned him more consistent condemnation as a gaudy liar than his retelling of his years in the mountains with the Rocky Mountain Fur Company. Generous readers might be inclined to attribute the many discrepancies in his story as much to the vagaries of a memory many years removed from the events in question and a conscious desire to fashion an entertaining and compelling narrative as to a full-fledged attempt at self-aggrandizement. If the result was something more in the fashion of a tall tale than an accurate historical record, then that, too, was in the best tradition of the West.

THE POISON TRAP

COLLECTING PELTS.

INTERIOR OF TRAPPERS LODGE

NOTHING BUT A CROW

STILL HUNTING THE MOOSE

SHOOTING A COUGAR

THE BEAVER TRAP

OTTERS FISHING

KILLING BUFFALO.

PROTECTING TRAPS

4

THE STORYTELLER

J IM BECKWOURTH'S SKILL as a raconteur was very much appreciated by those with whom he gathered around a campfire at the rendezvous in 1825 and in years to come. (Although some doubt persists as to exactly when Beckwourth arrived in the mountains, he was most certainly there by 1825 and was an enthusiastic participant in the revels at Henry's Fork.) Fur trappers led a life of almost unimaginable solitude and hardship, with few creature comforts and little in the way of what others might consider entertainment. The outsider who could enthrall his listeners over the embers of fire with a whopper of a yarn was therefore a valued companion, and the swapping of tall tales among friends eager to catch up with each other's escapades in the year since they had last been together was an essential and flavorsome component of the rendezvous.

At the rendezvous, a trapper tested his prowess at storytelling in the same fashion that he competed in the footraces, wrestling matches, drinking bouts, and shooting contests with which the mountain men also amused themselves. Among the mountain men, the term *gaudy liar*, which was so often applied to Beckwourth that it became virtually synonymous with his name, most likely did not carry the same scornful connotations that a generation of historians, beginning with the hallowed Francis Parkman, has imbued it. The term was equally as likely to have been one of respect, uttered among the amused, outraged howls of derision and snorts, guffaws, and chuckles of

The life of a mountain man, as illustrated in the October 17, 1868, issue of Harper's Weekly.

55

Perhaps the most famous of all the mountain men, Jim ("Gabe") Bridger was the discoverer of the Great Salt Lake in Utah. Like his friend Beckwourth, Bridger was not only a valued member of the Rocky Mountain Fur Company but an accomplished spinner of yarns.

bemusement that accompanied the preposterous ending of another outlandish, well-told tale. As such, it was more a compliment to the creative skill of the teller's tale than a dig at his veracity.

According to the historian Dale L. Morgan, one of the foremost chroniclers of the fur trade, "To be a gifted liar was as much part of mountain honor as hard drinking or straight shooting. Embroider your adventures, convert to your uses any handy odyssey, and spin it all out in the firelight, the only sin the sin of being dull." And Beckwourth's stories were never dull. He loved to talk, possessed a seemingly inexhaustible fund of yarns, and owned a musical, lilting voice that commanded and rewarded a listener's attention. "His language," according to one who heard him speak, "was much superior to that usually heard in the Rocky Mountains in his day."

Beckwourth's autobiography, which he dictated rather than wrote, was no doubt intended to follow in this tradition of oral storytelling. After all, mountain men were used to being disbelieved, even when they spoke the truth, especially by those back east.

In his later years, Jim Bridger, Beckwourth's friend and colleague in the Rocky Mountain Fur Company, lamented the failure of city folks to credit his tales of wilderness life. "They said I was the damndest liar that ever lived. That's what a mountain man gets for telling the truth," complained Bridger.

It is difficult to blame the skeptics, however, for so much of the mountain men's life was unbelievable. Who can fault the listeners who scoffed at John Colter's tales of a fantastic region, in what is now the northwest corner of Wyoming, of oozing tar pits, boiling springs, and sulphuric vents and thereby, for six decades, made "Colter's Hell" a geographic joke on par with the lost continent of Atlantis? (The laughing stopped when government surveyors in the early 1870s emerged from the same remote regions with photographs of the geysers and volcanic wonders of Yellowstone, which shortly thereafter was made the first national park in the world.) Or those who disregarded Bridger's assertion that in the course of his wanderings in 1825 he drank the salty waters of a great inland sea? (A little more than two decades later, large numbers of Mormon pioneers were coaxing crops from the desert sands surrounding the Great Salt Lake.) Town residents and city dwellers of the 19th century also found it difficult to believe that western expeditions sometimes had to halt for several days at a time to allow tremendous herds of buffalo, numbering hundreds of thousands of animals, to pass completely by.

Even those who might have been expected to know better were sometimes ill served by their skepticism. On their way west, Meriwether Lewis, William Clark, and the Corps of Discovery regularly discounted the stories they heard about the size, strength, speed, and ferocity of the grizzly bear, which then made virtually the entire West its domain. Yet after a couple of encounters, they were ready to change their tune. "I must confess that I do not like the gentlemen and had rather fight two Indians than one bear," Lewis was soon confiding to his journal, "gentlemen" being his newly respectful term for the magnificent bruin.

Faced with such widespread disbelief, mountain men relished the prospect of putting one over on the more gullible members of their audience. Bridger, for example, delighted in telling of the time he had been treed by a wolf pack. After a stand-off of several hours, all but one of the wolves departed and Bridger relaxed, certain that his lone nemesis would soon tire of waiting and seek out some easier prey. His confidence turned to terror, however, when he spotted the rest of the wolves returning, trotting slowly and herding a beaver in their midst. The enslaved rodent

Grizzly bears were just one of the many dangers that trappers encountered during their adventures in the American West. "I must confess that I do not like the gentlemen," noted Meriwether Lewis (opposite page), who along with William Clark commanded the Corps of Discovery, the most famous journey of exploration in the nation's history.

was then, according to Bridger, put to work gnawing down the tree in which he crouched. As the tree began to totter precariously and the wolves leaped and snapped their powerful jaws in anticipation, a fellow mountain man happened by and effected a rescue. (Dramatic and unlikely escapes were very much a part of the genre.)

Like literature, the best stories took on a higher reality above and beyond their fidelity to the real-life experience at their core. Their value lay in their illustration of a central truth about the life of a fur trapper—most frequently, the tremendous hardship it entailed—and the qualities of character that the life required, rather than in their literal correlation to actual reality. None was told more often, by Beckwourth and others, than the saga of Old Hugh Glass and the grizzly bear.

While traveling west with Andrew Henry from Fort Kiowa in September 1823, Glass absented himself from the main party to do a little hunting. (Dale Morgan records that it was said of him, as of Beckwourth and most mountain men, that "short of shooting him, it was difficult to get any obedience from him.") Along the Grand River, not far west of the Arikara villages, he was set upon and horribly mauled by a grizzly. His companions, when they found him, agreed that his death would come quickly; indeed, most were amazed that he had survived his wounds for any time at all.

After a day, Glass was still clinging to life. But his death seemed inevitable, and Henry and his men could not afford to wait for it. Winter would be arriving on the high plains soon, they still had many miles to go to reach Fort Henry, and the utmost caution had to be taken to avoid the still irate Arikaras. Henry asked for two volunteers to stay with Glass until he died or could travel again; they would be paid half a year's wages. Jim Bridger and Thomas Fitzpatrick stepped forward.

Henry proceeded onward to the Yellowstone and his fort, which he reached without great mishap. Bridger and Fitzgerald arrived there several days later, with the sad tale of Glass's death, his rifle, his knife, and several other personal effects.

Meanwhile, back near the Grand, Glass was experiencing a resurrection. Either out of panic at finding themselves alone in the wilderness—both were still comparative newcomers—impatience in awaiting what they regarded as the inevitable, or a mistaken interpretation of Glass's coma as death, Bridger and Fitzpatrick had abandoned their charge. He awoke several days later, weaponless and alone. He had been left only a flint and a razor.

Glass nursed himself at a creek nearby with wild berries and cold water for the next 10 days. Then he began crawling across the prairie. After a couple of days, he came across some wolves feeding on the carcass of a buffalo they had killed. Taking advantage of the prevailing wind, he used his flint to set the prairie grass afire and drive off the wolves and his razor to hack meat from the buffalo's bones, which he ate raw.

Trappers on the Prairie—Peace or War?, *a 19th-century lithograph by the prominent American printmakers Currier and Ives.* "I could always travel the road in safety while other men were attacked and killed," *Beckwourth said.* "The only way in which I could account for the marvel, was that I knew how to act the 'wolf.'"

Glass remained by the carcass for several more days, eating, slaking his thirst with the dead beast's blood, and gaining strength until he was able to walk. At first, he traveled less than a mile a day. His wounds bled with every step, and insects feasted on the raw flesh of his back. Still, miraculously, he grew stronger, feeding on berries and herbs and the occasional buffalo carcass. At last, a Sioux war party, on the move against their Arikara enemies, found him and brought him back to Fort Kiowa.

Vowing revenge on the men who had left him, Glass set out immediately for Fort Henry. He walked most of the way, alone. After six weeks, he arrived at the fort, only to find it abandoned, Henry having decided to move his post southwest to the Bighorn River. Apparently, Henry had left news of his new location either at his old fort or with the Indians, for Glass simply continued, undeterred, on his grim errand.

He arrived at Henry's new fort at the end of December, a little more than three months after his unfortunate encounter. Emaciated, spectral, and ghastly, he walked in on his fellow trappers as they were well into the carousing with which they would usher in the new year. The trappers could not believe their eyes; hesitantly, they reached out to touch Glass, as if to assure themselves that this was no apparition. Bridger, who was extremely superstitious, started as if he had seen a ghost.

"Young man," Glass solemnly intoned, "it is Glass that it is before you, the same that not content with leaving, you thought, to a cruel death upon the prairie, you robbed, helpless, as he was, of his rifle, his knife, of all with which he could hope to defend or save himself. . . . I swore an oath that I would be revenged on you, and the wretch who was with you, and I ever thought to have kept it. For this meeting I have braved the dangers of a long journey. . . . But I cannot take your life. . . . You have nothing to fear from me; go—you are free—for your youth I forgive you."

It took Glass six more months and countless more adventures to track down Fitzgerald, whom he found serving as a private in the Sixth Infantry at Fort Atkinson. There, after reclaiming his rifle, Glass told his enemy: "Go false man and answer to your conscience and your God. I have suffered enough in all reason by your perfidy. You was well paid to have remained with me until I should be able to walk. You promised to do so—or to wait my death and decently bury my remains. I heard the bargain. But enough; again I say, settle the matter with your own conscience and your God."

Few mountain men were the subjects of such fantastic adventures as Glass, but the toughness, self-reliance, ingenuity, and perseverance required of each by the day-to-day reality of his life in the mountains was scarcely less remarkable. By most accounts, in the daily exercise of his profession, Beckwourth, who spent most of his time between the Yellowstone River and the North Platte, along the Powder and the Bighorn, was one of the best of this solitary, hardy breed.

5

THE LIFE OF A
MOUNTAIN MAN

Mist in the Kanab Canyon, *a 19th-century painting by Thomas Moran. Beckwourth and the other mountain men would scavenge the land for food, at times subsisting on a diet of berries, nuts, and roots when there was no game in the area.*

MOST MOUNTAIN MEN, including Jim Beckwourth, generally worked alone or in pairs. The prime trapping seasons were from the onset of autumn until winter's ice and snow made movement in the mountains too difficult for work to continue, and in the early spring, when the ice first began to melt and an animal's winter fur was at its thickest. Little trapping was done in the brief mountain summer, one month of which was customarily devoted to the rendezvous.

Trappers were generally rather lightly equipped. Their most important pieces of equipment, by far, were their traps and rifle. The most desirable traps were made by Sewell Newhouse of Oneida, New York, and sold for between $12 and $16 apiece. They were set underwater in a pond, lake, creek, or swamp and baited with castoreum, the substance secreted by a beaver's scent glands. (Castoreum was also highly regarded as a remedy for a large variety of illnesses. Modern chemical analysis has shown that it contains large quanties of acetylsalicylic acid, the primary ingredient in aspirin and many other manufactured analgesics.) When an unsuspecting beaver stepped on a disk in the middle of the trap, steel jaws on either side clamped shut on its leg, and the unfortunate animal was pinioned underwater until it drowned. The trapper, making his rounds, had then only to collect the carcass.

Equally as valued by the mountain man was his rifle. The weapon of choice was manufactured by the Hawken brothers of St. Louis and was advertised as being accurate and powerful enough to take down a grizzly, buffalo, or Blackfoot at 200 yards. The trapper relied on his gun to keep himself in food during the long autumn, winter, and spring months. He might bring with him from the rendezvous a little flour, tea, coffee, and salt, but mountain men were primarily hunters and survived on a carnivorous diet of buffalo, deer, elk, and antelope meat.

Beckwourth's long years in the mountains attest to his skill with a gun; poor hunters simply did not make it. Like the rest, he would have subsisted on roots, berries, nuts, tree bark, and crickets and other insects during lean times. It was not unheard of for mountain men to be reduced to gnawing on leather and their boots in the dead of winter.

The mountain man's other possessions usually consisted of no more than several knives, ammunition, gunpowder, flints, tobacco, and a pipe. Those who could read might carry with them a volume of Shakespeare or, as in Jedediah Smith's case, a Bible. Jim Bridger, who was illiterate, nevertheless loved to listen to Shakespeare being read aloud. In his later years, when he had come out of the mountains, Bridger traded a yoke of oxen for an edition of Shakespeare and paid a local youth $40 a month to read it to him. He became fond of declaiming the immortal Bard's works, often seasoning the poetry with creative oaths he had learned in the Rockies.

The frigid winter months were spent in an improvised shelter, usually camouflaged so as to protect it from the eyes of wandering Indians, where the mountain man spent most of his days at the tedious work of preparing his furs to be sold. Often, these "shantees" resembled Indian tipis, as described by the mountain man Rufus Sage:

> His shantee faces a huge fire, and is formed of skins carefully extended over an arched frame-work of slender poles, which are bent in the form of a semicircle and kept to their places by inserting their extremities in the ground. Near this is his 'graining block,' planted aslope, for the ease of the operative in preparing his skins for the finishing process in the art of dressing; and not far removed is a stout frame, contrived from four pieces of timber, so tied together as to leave a square of sufficient dimensions for the required, in which, perchance, a skin is stretched to its fullest extension, and the hardy mountaineer is busily engaged in rubbing it with a rough stone or 'scraper,' to fit for the manufacture of clothing.

At night, the mountain man bedded down on the ground near the fire and wrapped himself in buffalo robes. Some warmed themselves with the company of an Indian woman purchased for that purpose. The practice was widespread, and Beckwourth was extremely fond of such female companionship. The going rate for women of the Mandan tribe, who were especially prized for their beauty, was two horses, a gun with enough ammunition and powder for a year, and several gallons of whiskey.

Indian "wives" notwithstanding, a common consequence of the mountain man's constant exposure to cold, and especially of their frequent immersion in icy water in setting and gathering their traps, was arthritis. Many mountain men found their joints aching and crippled at an extremely young age. Rheumatism had simply to be endured. (Some mountain men recommended rubbing stiffened joints with petroleum that oozed from a spring near present-day Lander, Wyoming.)

More acute medical crises required the trappers to do their own doctoring. Wounds and rattlesnake bites were cauterized with gunpowder. Buffalo gall (the animal's bile) was cited as an effective remedy for a variety of ailments. Broken limbs had to be set immediately without benefit of anesthesia, except perhaps for a jug of whiskey. Gangrenous limbs had to be amputated, usually with a handsaw and a butcher knife but also without anesthesia.

A particularly redoubtable mountain man named Thomas Smith attained the status of legend by amputating his badly mangled right leg himself; he was known thereafter as Pegleg. Bridger walked around for three years with an arrowhead imbedded in his back and neck muscles until a fellow trapper, Marcus Whitman, volunteered to carve it out. Most mountain men, in fact, bore an array of scars and badly healed wounds as testament to their years in the wilderness. For some, such as Jedediah Smith, long hair served a cosmetic purpose: to hide the damage done by a grizzly bear's claws. Trapping was, all in all, a calling that aged a man quickly.

The mountain man's appearance was usually as singular as his way of life. According to Rufus Sage,

His skin from constant exposure, assumes a hue almost as dark as that of the Aborigine, and his features and physical structure attain a rough and hardy cast. His hair, through inattention, becomes long, coarse, and bushy, and loosely dangles upon his shoulders. His head is surmounted by a low crowned wool-hat, or a rude substitute of his own manufacture. His clothes are of buckskin, gaily fringed at the seams with strings of the same material, cut and made in a fashion peculiar to himself and associates. The deer and buffalo furnish the required covering for his feet, which he fabricates at the impulse of want. His waist is encircled with a belt of leather, holding encased his butcher-knife and pistols—

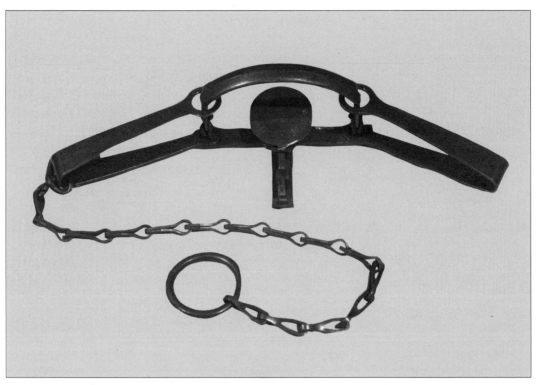

while from his neck is suspended a bullet pouch securely fastened to the belt in front. . . . With . . . a good rifle placed in his hands . . . the reader will have before him a correct likeness of a genuine mountaineer when fully equipped.

Even among such exotics, Beckwourth's appearance set him apart. Six feet tall, rangy and muscular, a frequent victor in the footraces and wrestling matches at the rendezvous, he wore his thick black hair down to his waist. He was dark-skinned and dark-eyed, but some of his contemporaries noted that there was nothing in his appearance to suggest he was of black ancestry; many assumed that he was part Spanish or Indian.

Ornamentation added to his striking appearance. Beckwourth loved to bedeck himself with gold chains, often braided his hair or tied it at his neck with colorful silk ribbons, and had both ears pierced

A fur trapper such as Beckwourth captured beavers by setting his traps in a lake, pond, or river after baiting them with castoreum, an oil secreted by the rodent's scent glands. A beaver would be drawn to the trap by the castoreum, then activate the device by stepping on the disk in the middle, causing the steel jaws to spring shut on the beaver's leg and pinning the animal underwater until it drowned.

in several places to accommodate his collection of earrings. At the rendezvous, he often paraded around in the handsome embroidered and beaded leggings and robes made by the Crow Indians.

For Beckwourth and his fellow mountain men, the only real reward for their difficult and lonesome life was its living. William Ashley and his like may have ridden away from the rendezvous as wealthy men, but few mountain men ever grew rich. Most of their year's earnings were generally spent paying off the debts incurred in outfitting themselves; the remainder was usually gone by the end of the rendezvous, frittered away on liquor and the "foofaraw" in which they delighted. It is unlikely that many of them would have taken consolation in the knowledge that their wanderings were preparing the way for the advance of American settlement; most were in the mountains because, for one reason or another, they found "civilization" too confining.

Their compensation was the matchless experience of exploring a land of incomparable natural beauty, one rich in wildlife and treated respectfully by its native inhabitants, and the certainty that whoever came after them would never experience the land in quite the same way as those of their countrymen who had been the first to lay eyes on it. For men like Beckwourth, their circumstances— harsh as they were—were their own reward; such experiences were what, after all, they had come west to find. To camp alone by a fresh mountain stream, with only the innumerable glittering stars and the howling of wolves as company, was a privilege, not a hardship. For such men, said Ashley, "their privations in the end became sources of amusement to them."

One senses, in Beckwourth's musings about the settlers who followed the mountain men west, his pride in the life he and his companions lived.

When I recurred to my own adventures, I would smile at the comparison of their sufferings with what myself and other men of the mountains had really endured in former times. The forts that now afford protection to the traveler were built by ourselves at the constant peril of our lives, amid Indian tribes nearly double their present numbers. Without wives and children to comfort us on our lonely way; without well-furnished wagons to resort to when hungry, no roads before us but trails temporarily made; our clothing consisting of the skins of animals that had fallen before our unerring rifles, and often whole days on insufficient rations, or entirely without food; occasionally our whole party on guard the entire night, and our strength deserting us through unceasing watching and fatigue; these are sufferings that made theirs appear trivial, and ours surpass in magnitude my own powers of relation. ❧

6

AMONG THE CROW

━━━━ ⋅◖◗⋅ ━━━━

A T THE 1828 rendezvous, a wizened trapper named Caleb Greenwood, with whom Jim Beckwourth enjoyed a friendship based on jesting and put-ons, spent much of his time regaling some Crow Indians with stories of Beckwourth's prowess as a hunter, rider, and fighter. (Indians regularly attended the rendezvous in order to trade. Although peace usually prevailed, at least one rendezvous degenerated into a shoot-out between the Americans and the Indians.) The Crow were generally quite welcoming to American fur trappers, possibly because their great enemies, the Sioux and the Blackfoot, were so hostile. Certainly the heroics in battle against the Blackfoot that Greenwood attributed to Beckwourth (tales that Beckwourth echoed in his autobiography) impressed the Crow.

Some historians believe that the Crow's fascination with Beckwourth stemmed as well from their high regard for Edward Rose, like Beckwourth a black man of mixed blood. Rose had been visiting the Crow since 1807, when he made his first journey up the Missouri with Manuel Lisa, one of the pioneers of the fur trade. Since that time, Rose had been made a Crow war chief and had taken a number of Crow wives, with whom he had had several children.

Sue Beckwourth, the last in a succession of Beckwourth's many Native American wives. He also married two non-Indians, Elizabeth Ledbetter and Luisa Sandoval.

71

Beckwourth joined the Crow Indians, he said, "to gratify a youthful thirst for adventure; I had traversed the vastnesses of the far Rocky Mountains in summer heats and winter frosts; I had encountered savage beasts and wild men." The Crow were just as intrigued with Beckwourth and made him a war chief.

Many Indian tribes preferred dealing with blacks, whom they found inherently more sympathetic, than with whites. For this very reason, according to James Stevenson, a 19th-century ethnologist who spent more than 30 years living with various Indian tribes and recording their customs, the more experienced fur trappers often made use of black men as translators and mediators. Rose spoke more than a dozen Indian languages, but the key to the esteem in which he was held by the Indians was his mastery of their wilderness skills. A contemporary wrote of him that "he was as cunning as a prairie wolf. He was a perfect woodsman. He could endure any kind of fatigue and privation as well as the best trained Indians. He studied men. There was nothing that an Indian could do, that Rose did not make himself master of. He knew all that Indians knew. He was a great man in his situation." Apparently, Beckwourth's skills were comparable to Rose's, an aptitude the Crow attributed in some part to their shared racial background.

It is one of the many contradictions in Beckwourth's life that the Indians' admiration for his blackness does not accord with the assertions that he took some pains to hide his racial identity, or with the recollections of some of his contemporaries that indicate by appearance Beckwourth was not necessarily identifiable as a black man. Many more contemporary accounts, however, emphasize that Beckwourth was a black man, with the term *mulatto* being frequently used, which would seem to indicate that his black ancestry was no secret.

In any event, the Crow were fascinated by Beckwourth, and they were delighted to learn from the mischievous Greenwood that Beckwourth was part Crow. Some time in the winter months following the rendezvous of 1828, Beckwourth decided to take advantage of Greenwood's prank. While working with a large party headed by Robert Campbell, which was trapping in the vicinity of the Powder River, Beckwourth and Jim Bridger detached themselves to trap in some streams they knew about. (By this time, Bridger's panicky abandonment of Old Hugh Glass some five years earlier had been forgiven by all; he enjoyed an unparalleled reputation as a mountain man, one who, in the words of a contemporary, "possessed a complete and absolute understanding of the Indian character in all its different phases.... His bravery was unquestionable, his horsemanship equally so.")

After splitting with Bridger at the fork of one of the watercourses near Powder River, Beckwourth "blundered" into a herd of Crow ponies and allowed himself to be taken "captive." Fully expecting a warm reception because of the reputation that Greenwood had made for him, he was unalarmed by his "fate." But poor Bridger, who was watching from the top of a hill on the far side of the stream's other fork, was terrified for his friend.

In his autobiography, Beckwourth states that Bridger believed the captors were Cheyenne, not the friendly Crow, and intended to "sacrifice me in the most approved manner their savage propensities could suggest." Upon "seeing clearly that he could oppose no resistance to my captors," Bridger "made all speed to the camp, and communicated the painful news of my death. . . . All were plunged in gloom. All pronounced my funeral eulogy; all my daring encounters were spoken of to my praise. My fortunate escapes, my repeated victories were applauded in memory of me; the loss of their best hunter, of their kind and ever-obliging friend, was deplored by all."

Beckwourth, of course, had carefully orchestrated his own "capture," and as he had expected, he received an especially warm welcome from the Crow. His motives in joining the Indians remain uncertain, although instances of trappers adopting an Indian way of life were not at all uncommon in the West. In some ways, the existence of the free trapper, with his nomadic dependence on hunting and game and his proximity to nature, had much in common with that of the Indians; by being adopted into a tribe, an individual could enjoy the benefits of community without sacrificing his freedom and could even maintain his former way of life. Beckwourth, for example, continued to act as a fur trader and trapper during his years with the Crow.

Adoption by an Indian tribe could even be an economic boon for a trapper, for who knew better the lands where the beaver made its home than the native human inhabitants? Certainly this motive played no small part in Beckwourth's decision to join the Crow. "I said to myself," he wrote, " 'I can trap in their streams unmolested, and derive more profit under their protection than if among my own men, exposed incessantly to assassination and alarm.' " Before leaving his colleagues for the Indians, Beckwourth signed a promissory note for $275, payable in beaver skins; he most likely incurred the indebtedness in exchange for trapping equipment advanced him.

Perhaps the aspect of Indian life that held the most allure for young American men was its liberated sexuality. Among the Indians of the Great Plains, sexual behavior was governed by few of the legal and religious restraints that prevailed in American society. Beckwourth was most enchanted by the sexual freedom he found among the Indians, and within days of his arrival he was so enjoying the "untutored caresses" of the first of his many Indian "wives" that he determined to make his stay an extended one. Like many blacks who lived among the Indians, Beckwourth discovered his new existence to be a liberation from the stigmas attached to his skin color by white society.

According to Woodson Carter, one of the pioneers in the field of black history, blacks and Indians had been maintaining an interrelationship for centuries, forming "one of the longest unwritten chapters in the history of the United States." In the South, escaped black slaves found haven among the Indians. In the West, blacks who lived with the Indians were able to find a degree of personal freedom largely unavailable to them elsewhere in the United States and its territories.

How large a part such considerations played in Beckwourth's decision to "become" an Indian remains unknown, but if true, the reports that indicate he was essentially trying to "pass" as a white man would indicate that he felt profoundly the burden of his black heritage. Indeed, the illustrations that accompanied the first edition of his autobiography portray him as white. Moreover, the book makes no mention of his mother's ancestry, and nowhere does he say anything to indicate he was part black. Critics have pointed to these omissions as examples of Beckwourth's propensity for lying, yet his silence on the matter—bespeaking either shame, confusion, unease, denial, or circumspection—suggests that his

racial identity had been a matter not without consequence, most likely painful, to him.

It is even possible that Beckwourth's departure
from the Rocky Mountain Fur Company was has-
tened by some sort of racial insult. He relates that a
quarrel and fistfight—ending just short of gunplay—
arising from the scornful reception of one of his tales
provided the pretext for his deciding to go to the
Crow. The narrative tone of this incident is notice-
ably devoid of the tongue-in-cheek humor that per-
meates the rest of his autobiography; Beckwourth's
anger is palpable. "I could have taken his expression
in jest, for we were very free in our sallies upon one
another," he said, "but in this particular instance I
saw his intention was to insult me, and I allowed my
passion to overcome my reflection."

Clearly, Beckwourth felt himself much more appreciated by the Crow than by his free trapper
comrades. He said of his reception by the Indians:
"The faithful fellows little thought that, while they
were lamenting my untimely fall, I was being hugged
and kissed to death by a whole lodge of near and dear
Crow relatives, and that I was being welcomed with
a public reception fully equal in intensity, though not
in extravagance, to that accorded to the victor of
Waterloo on his triumphant entry into Paris."

For a time, Beckwourth seems to have found great
happiness among the Crow, whom the mountain men
believed to be the most admirable Indians of the
Great Plains. The Crow were renowned for their
horsemanship, at which Beckwourth also excelled,
and for the beadwork and craftsmanship of their robes
and leggings, which Beckwourth delighted in wearing. They were also the foremost thieves on the High
Plains.

Among the Crow, no moral stigma was attached
to stealing. Even after the Crow turned more hostile
toward whites, their animosity usually took the form

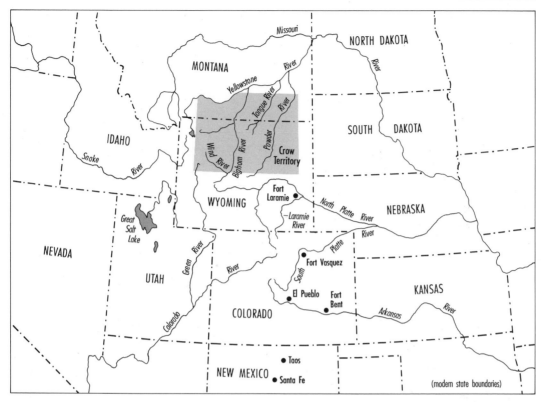

of theft rather than warfare. "This they frankly explain," said Bill Gordon, a fur trader contemporary of Beckwourth's, "by telling us that if they killed, we would not come back, & they would lose the chance of stealing from us. They have no shame about stealing and will talk over their past thefts to you with all possible frankness and indifference."

To pilfer a pony was for the Crow a mark of high honor, a means by which young men proved their valor. According to Gordon, the Crow practice of stealing horses from fur trappers and then returning them for a "reward" was "so common that it hardly interrupts friendship." Beckwourth, in dictating his autobiography, was circumspect about his participation in Crow horse-stealing raids. Nevertheless, one of the many nicknames the Crow bestowed on him was Enemy of Horses.

Beckwourth spent nearly a quarter of a century adventuring in parts of what is now Colorado and Wyoming.

The Crow's rustling skills apparently enabled Beckwourth to enact a measure of revenge for whatever grudge he seemed to bear his former colleagues and company. In the autumn of 1833, Thomas Fitzpatrick led a party of 25 to 30 fur trappers into the valley of the Bighorn River, where they were relieved of all their horses, equipment, and furs by a band of Crow warriors. Beckwourth is believed to have been the mastermind of this operation, especially because many of the furs wound up being sold by the American Fur Company, whose employ he had entered some time shortly after joining the Crow.

Beckwourth's account of his years with the Crow contains some of the most blood-soaked passages of his narrative, which the eminent historian of the West Bernard DeVoto believed "may well the goriest book" in American literature. According to Beckwourth, the Crow were on the warpath unceasingly against their Indian enemies, and he was in the thick of every encounter. His account of a Crow assault on a Blackfoot war party holed up in a seemingly impregnable "fortress" made by a natural granite formation is typical. After rallying the cowed Crow warriors with an impassioned speech—a detail verified by an American eyewitness, Zenas Leonard—Beckwourth, said Leonard, "leaped from the rock on which he had been standing, and, looking neither to the right nor to the left made for the fort as fast as he could run."

Beckwourth recalled of this encounter that "the carnage for some minutes was fearful. . . . The clash of battle-axes, and the yells of the opposing combatants was truly appalling. . . . The interior of this huge rock was concave, and the blood all ran to the center, where it formed a pool, which emitted a sickening smell as the warm vapor ascended to our nostrils. . . . Victims who were making away with their bowels ripped open were instantly felled with the battle-axe and stilled in death." DeVoto, whose

knowledge of the literature of the West was encyclopedic, asserted that he knew of no book in which as many Indians were killed as Beckwourth's.

Such exploits earned Beckwourth another Indian name—Bloody Arm—and acknowledgment as a war chief of the Crow. The appellation "chief" was often misunderstood by American settlers, who equated it with "monarch" or "king." More accurately, chief was a position of leadership, influence, and respect, but in most tribes the authority of the chief was far from absolute. Decisions were usually made by consensus, with the chief exercising influence through the force of his character and the esteem in which he was held rather than through any power inherent in his position.

Among the Crow, for example, there were many war chiefs. One could earn the designation in a variety of manners: by striking an enemy with the hand in battle; by stealing his weapon in hand-to-hand combat; by stealing an enemy's horse from a guarded corral or enclosure; or by leading a successful raid. Beckwourth's status as war chief meant nothing more than that he was entitled to participate in the tribe's councils and that the words he spoke there would be listened to with a certain amount of re-

A group of Crow Indians form a war party. "In justice to the Crows," Beckwourth said, "I must say, that other tribes were generally the aggressors, until the policy was forced upon me of endeavoring to 'conquer a peace.' I thought, if I could make the Crow nation a terror to all their neighbors, that their antagonists would be reduced to petition for peace, and then turn their battle-axes into beaver-traps, and their lances into hunting-knives."

spect. Whatever other influence he exercised was attributable to the power of his personality and character rather than his title.

Such distinctions were usually beyond the comprehension of outside observers of the Crow, and, rightly or wrongly, Beckwourth was held responsible for the incessant warfare in which the Crow engaged while he was with them. In truth, the Crow hardly needed Beckwourth to incite them, as their animosity toward the Sioux, the Blackfoot, and the Cheyenne was boundless. In his memoirs, Beckwourth asserted that the Crow were usually the aggrieved party in these encounters, as "other tribes were continually attacking the Crow, killing their braves, and stealing their horses."

There is little doubt that at the time the Crow were feeling considerable pressure. White incursion had forced the much more numerous Sioux and Arapaho westward from their traditional lands into Absaroka, which is how the Crow referred to their territory. Their response, in Beckwourth's words, was to "conquer a peace"—that is, to make themselves such a terror that none would dare treat them with impunity.

And to this end, of course, Beckwourth related, his own services were indispensable. "Disgusted at the repeated acts of cruelty I witnessed, I often resolved to leave these wild children of the forest and return to civilized life," he said many years later. "But before I could act upon my decision, another scene of strife would occur, and the Enemy of Horses was always the first sought by the tribe."

Beckwourth's assessment of his importance to the tribe was probably not an exaggeration. Charles Larpenteur, who spent 40 years in the region as a fur trader and trapper, recalled that Beckwourth was the "great brave warrior among the Crows," and many of his contemporaries echoed this evaluation. His superiors at the American Fur Company certainly concurred.

The company had hired Beckwourth to persuade the Crow to trap furs and trade them exclusively with it, but the tribe proved more interested in stealing horses and fighting, which they regarded as much more appropriate pursuits for Indians of their stature. Beckwourth was forced to acknowledge this state of affairs in explaining to his employers why he was unable to restrain his Indian friends: "An old warrior despises the sight of a trap; hunting buffalo, even, does not afford him excitement enough. Nothing but war or a horsestealing raid is a business worth attending to, and the chief who seeks to control this predilection too far loses popularity."

Beckwourth's rueful words about the comparative pleasures of warfare and trapping seem to apply as much to himself as to his Indian friends. With the Crow's rambunctiousness playing havoc with the entire fur trade, the American Fur Company terminated Beckwourth's employment in 1836, and he left Absaroka sometime shortly afterward. The specific reasons for his departure remain obscure—the end of his job, perhaps, or the dissension among the Crow, with himself at the center, which some contemporaries spoke of—yet his leavetaking was timely.

As always in his adventurous life, Beckwourth was in the forefront of historical change. With silk having replaced beaver fur as the material of choice for dandies and ladies of fashion, the great age of the fur trade, and the era of the mountain men, was fast coming to an end. Soon, the business of settlement of the West would begin, with far more monumental consequences for the land and its native peoples than the fur trade.

7

FIGHTING THE SEMINOLE

◆◆◆

AS IF TO herald the destruction of the West that was yet to come, in 1837 and 1838 a smallpox epidemic ravaged the Missouri River tribes. The Sioux, the Mandan, the Blackfoot, the Assiniboin, and the Pawnee were especially hard hit. Some estimates place the deaths at three-quarters of the members of these tribes, but worse was still in store for these peoples. (A long-lived rumor, still repeated in some sources, that the plague was intentionally brought to the Blackfoot in the form of an infected blanket by an inoculated Jim Beckwourth has been conclusively demonstrated to be baseless.)

After leaving Absaroka, Beckwourth drifted back to St. Louis, but after so many years of breathing the mountain air he found city life confining. The several months he spent there were a depressing period of desultory carousing and drunken streetfighting. Release came in the form of words of advice from his old fur-trading colleague William Sublette, who advised him to volunteer for the expeditionary force

A 19th-century engraving of U.S. Army troops engaging the Seminole at the Battle of Okeechobee in central Florida. Beckwourth participated briefly in the Second Seminole War in 1837 and 1838.

then being organized to take part in the United States's ongoing war with the Seminole Indians in Florida.

Florida, Sublette told Beckwourth, would be a welcome change for him. It was a "delightful country," and Beckwourth would "find a wide difference between the cold regions of the Rocky Mountains and the genial and salubrious South." Moreover, Beckwourth would probably be able to recruit several of his old friends to join him. With the decline in the fur trade, there were a lot of down-at-the-heels free trappers roaming the streets and saloons of St. Louis.

With bullets and legislation, the United States had been fighting the war against the Seminole since 1817. The tribe was an offshoot of several southeastern Indian groups that fled to Florida to escape the expansion of American settlement. In Florida, they were joined by large numbers of runaway slaves, who were harbored by the tribe and intermarried with its members.

The Seminole War, which is usually divided into two parts by historians, was caused by the insatiable desire of American settlers for more land and the desire of southern planters to reclaim their lost slaves. Between 1817 and 1821, U.S. forces under General Andrew Jackson drove the Seminole from their well-ordered agricultural villages into the swampy thickets and marshes of central Florida. By terms of a peace treaty forced upon them in 1823, the Seminole were made to exchange 30 million acres of their fertile former lands for a sandy, marshy reservation of 5 million acres in the middle part of the future state.

This capitulation was not enough. The desire of American settlers for land in Florida and elsewhere in the South continued to grow, and in 1830, Jackson, who had become president of the United States, signed the Indian Relocation Act. By the terms of

General Andrew Jackson led a 2,000-man army into battle against the Seminole Indians in the First Seminole War. Subsequently elected the seventh president of the United States, he finished his second term in office around the time that Beckwourth volunteered to take part in the Second Seminole War.

this legislation, all the Indians of the Southeast were to be relocated—forcibly, if need be—beyond the Mississippi, to what was then called Indian Territory (essentially, the future state of Oklahoma).

The Seminole resistance to this relocation, under the inspired generalship of a war chief named Osceola, caused the outbreak of the Second Seminole War in 1835. Making clever use of his superior knowledge of the singular topography of central Florida, with its humid swamps and impenetrable thickets, Osceola and his followers bedeviled the troops sent to roust them. By the time both parts of the Seminole War were concluded, it would be the most expensive Indian conflict in the history of the United States.

Senator Thomas Hart Benton of Missouri made it possible for Beckwourth and other experienced frontiersmen to participate in the Second Seminole War. Benton convinced Congress that the U.S. Army would wrap up the war quickly if it received the help of a volunteer cavalry regiment.

The ever-mounting cost of the confrontation was what precipitated Beckwourth's involvement. Enraged at the war's drain on the federal treasury, Senator Thomas Hart Benton of Missouri called for the formation of a brigade of volunteers from his state to fight the Seminole. According to Benton, the army's troubles in Florida could be attributed to the inexperience of its members, most of whom were easterners. What was needed were old western hands, experienced in tracking and fighting Indians, and there was no better place to find such men than St. Louis.

It might seem unusual that Beckwourth would volunteer for action in a war conducted, at least in part, against former slaves. But there is no evidence that the issue troubled him, even though the presence of former slaves among the Indians again played a large factor in the government's decision to act against the Seminole. "This, you may be assured, is a negro and not an Indian war," said General Sidney Thomas Jesup, commander of the U.S. forces in Florida.

How Beckwourth felt about this aspect of the engagement is simply impossible to say. Certainly, despite his happiness with the Crow, he was untroubled at the prospect of making war against Indians. Even while with the Crow, he would say later, he had been serving American interests: "I fought in their behalf against the most relentless enemies of the white man. If I chose to become an Indian while living among them, it concerned no person but myself; and by doing so, I saved more life and property for the white man than a whole regiment of United States regulars could have done at the same time." This explanation may contain as well some insight into Beckwourth's feelings about fighting against other blacks; like other sections of his autobiography, it seems to indicate that the author is identifying himself with the "white man."

Beckwourth's time in Florida lasted only several months, from late 1837 through the start of the new year. For most of that period, he was employed as a muleskinner and messenger attached to the army, with his most noteworthy adventure being his presence at the Battle of Okeechobee. There a combination of U.S. soldiers and Missouri volunteers won an ultimately indecisive victory over Osceola, who had taken refuge in the swampy wilderness near central Florida's great lake.

The landscape did not greatly appeal to Beckwourth, and neither did his duty, which was insufficiently action-filled. The life he had known with the Crow was still in his blood; all this slogging through the mire contained none of the exhilaration of galloping across the Plains on horseback on a raid against the Pawnees. He lamented that the Seminole "had no horses worth stealing," and by early 1838 he had resolved to leave Florida to find adventure, "even if it was no better than borrowing horses of the Blackfeet." ◐

8

WANDERLUST

◄◊►

JIM BECKWOURTH RETURNED to St. Louis in the summer of 1838, but he was destined to remain in the boisterous river city for just five days. Despite his words about the disdain a warrior feels when asked to take up his traps, he decided to try his hand once again at the fur trade. This time, he would be working for his old friends Andrew Sublette, younger brother of William, and Louis Vasquez, a Rocky Mountain Fur Company veteran.

After a short voyage up the Missouri to the city of Independence, the trappers headed southwest by land along the Kansas and South Platte rivers, intending to take advantage of the less heavily trapped ranges of the southern Rockies and the still-thriving trade with New Mexico, which was then governed by Mexico. Beckwourth usually rode far out in front of the caravan of wagons, acting as scout. He trusted in his superior wilderness instincts—what he called his ability to "act the wolf"—to prevent the Indians from attacking him.

Vasquez had established a fort about a mile from present-day Platteville, Colorado, on the South Platte. Beckwourth was placed in charge there while his partners moved on to establish other posts. After a number of subordinates proved unable to locate the Cheyenne, with whom Beckwourth wished to establish commerce in buffalo robes, he set out in search of the Indians himself.

At their first meeting, Beckwourth attempted to awe the Cheyenne with his bravery, explaining that

This portrait of Beckwourth was printed in the first edition of his autobiography, The Life and Adventures of James P. Beckwourth, Mountaineer, Scout, Pioneer, and Chief of the Crow Nation.

he was a fugitive from the Crow, exiled because he had killed a great Crow chief, and that he had "come to the Cheyennes, who are the bravest people in the mountains," because he did not want to be "killed by any of the inferior tribes." His tone was reckless, intended to impress his listeners with his disdain for his own well-being. "I have come here to be killed by the Cheyennes, cut up, and thrown out for their dogs to eat, so that they may say they have killed a great Crow chief," Beckwourth said, much to the amusement of William Bent, who was with the Cheyenne at the time.

"You are certainly bereft of your senses," said Bent, who had long enjoyed a monopoly on trade with the Indians in the area and was not particularly fond of competitors. "The Indians will make sausage meat of you."

Yet the Indians welcomed Beckwourth, perhaps because of his audacious oratory, but more likely because he was willing to provide them with their most desired of American products: whiskey. In time, the introduction of alcoholic beverages to the Native populations of the West would become the single most devastating legacy of the fur trade. Native Americans have a genetic intolerance for alcohol that makes its physical and psychological effects especially destructive.

While with the Crow, whose abstinence from liquor was the primary reason for the great admiration the fur trappers felt for them, Beckwourth had taken great pride in ensuring that alcohol was never brought among them. But by the time he went among the Cheyenne, he had grown more cynical. The Cheyenne, he argued, had already become accustomed to consuming alcoholic beverages. He was a trader, charged with making money for his employees; his customers wanted whiskey, so he would provide it. As he put it, "The sale of liquor is one of the more profitable branches of a trader's business, and since the appetite for the vile potion had already been created, my personal influence in the matter was very slight. . . . If I had refused to sell it to the Indians, plenty more traders would have furnished it to them . . . and my conscientious scruples . . . would deprive my employers of a very considerable profit."

And the profits were considerable, allowing Vazquez and Sublette to sell out and forcing Beckwourth to move on. He engaged in a number of trading ventures in and around Colorado and New Mexico, some as a self-proprietor, some as an employee of the Bents. His chief provison of barter continued to be whiskey, despite a moving speech on its pernicious effects on the Cheyenne that he heard delivered by a chief named Porcupine Bear: "Our fires begin to burn dim, and will soon go out entirely. . . . I am ready to die. I will go and sit with my fathers in the spirit land, where I shall soon point down to the last expiring fire of the Cheyennes, and when they inquire the cause of this decline of their people, I will tell them with a straight tongue that it was the fire-water of the trader that put it out."

Profits from the trade in alcohol and furs enabled Beckwourth, for a short time, to establish a general store in Taos. There he courted and married Luisa Sandoval, about whom next to nothing is known, except that in October 1842 she accompanied him north to the Arkansas River in south-central Colorado, where he built a trading post. "In a very short time," Beckwourth recalled, he "was joined by fifteen to twenty free trappers, with their families." An adobe fort was constructed, cabins sprung up around Beckwourth's lean-to, which was both shelter and trading post, and a little community was established, which its denizens named Pueblo. It soon became one of the most infamous outposts of the West, a lawless, dissolute place notorious for its citizens' consumption of Taos Lightning—an incendiary blend of grain alcohol, red pepper, and gunpowder—and their predilection for settling all disputes with knives and guns.

Historian David Lavender has characterized Pueblo in its early days "as a collecting spot for the scum of the mountains." Beckwourth might well himself have agreed with that characterization as regarded Old Bill Williams, an eccentric mountain man, fond of wearing war paint and reputed to engage in cannibalism. After Williams called him a "low-down half-breed nigger Frenchman," Beckwourth tried to cut his throat. Williams, however, knocked Beckwourth senseless with a single blow from a rifle butt.

Shortly thereafter, the ever-restless Beckwourth decided to press on. Blithely abandoning Luisa and their infant daughter, he signed on 15 men, loaded the many horses he had obtained from the Cheyenne through the sale of whiskey with trade goods, and lit out for California. His destination was Los Angeles, where he planned to indulge his "new passion for trade."

With his usual propensity for adventure, Beckwourth arrived just in time for the beginnings of the Bear Flag Rebellion. Oso, the Spanish word for grizzly bear, was the name that the many American mountain men then resident in California, who were eager to detach the fertile territory from Mexican rule, took for themselves. A likeness of a grizzly bear also graced the flag the Osos adopted as their emblem.

Beckwourth jumped right into the tumult. If one accepts his own account (many historians have not), he joined the Osos, in whose number he found his former partner in mischief Caleb Greenwood, during their assault on the Mexican stronghold at Cahuenga. Certain chroniclers also credit Beckwourth with serving as a guide to John Frémont, the famed American

A man of many occupations, Beckwourth took on a new job in 1846, when he became a messenger for the U.S. Army. Carrying communications from one military installation to another in the Southwest, he usually traveled more than 700 miles on horseback every three weeks.

explorer known as the Pathfinder, who was then in California for the purpose of abetting the American effort there.

But Beckwourth's greatest contribution to the American cause, as he saw it, came upon his departure from California. With "five trusty Americans," he "collected"—that is, stole—a total of 2,000 horses from several Mexican-owned haciendas surrounding Los Angeles and drove them back with him to Pueblo. The proceeds from the sale of these four-footed spoils of war were used to purchase a saloon and hotel in Santa Fe, where for a price one could buy a glass of Taos Lightning, entry into a card game, the affection of a young woman, and a room for an evening or an hour.

Lewis Garrard, a 17-year-old adventurer who met Beckwourth at this time, described him as a "large, good-humored fellow" of infectious high spirits and was especially impressed, as was almost everyone who met the voluble mountain man, by his powers of conversation, which Garrard referred to as his "characteristic colloquy." Beckwourth's establishment, according to Garrard, was the "best furnished saloon" in Santa Fe, the "grand resort for liquor-imbibing, monte-playing, and fandango-disposed American men and officers."

According to some New Mexicans, Beckwourth supplemented his earnings from the hotel by stealing and selling horses and mules, although he claimed this was all a misunderstanding. What he was actually doing, he said, was carrying out a commission given him by the U.S. Army to reclaim stolen pack animals and mounts and return them to their rightful owners, who quite naturally provided him with a monetary reward in gratitude for the restoration of their lost property.

The war between Mexico and the United States over the Southwest, which began in 1846, gave Beckwourth another sideline. He was employed often by the army as a messenger to carry communications between various military installations, particularly Santa Fe and Fort Leavenworth, in Kansas—a trip of more than 700 miles, across mountain and prairie, that Beckwourth, on horseback, regularly made in about three weeks.

Like all of Beckwourth's occupations, these were short lived. In the late summer of 1848, he decided once again to go to California. His motivation seems to have been the wanderlust that was the one sustaining element of his unpredictable character rather than the extremely communicable contagion—gold fever—that was driving so many other Americans westward that same year. After making his way west to Los Angeles and then north to Monterey as a civilian member, probably a guide, of a war department caravan, he hired on as a dispatch rider between Dana's Ranch, near present-day Santa Maria, and Monterey.

The military authorities in California, which, like New Mexico, the United States had recently won from Mexico, had just established the first mail service on the Pacific Coast. The service connected

San Diego with San Francisco; Beckwourth and his fellow couriers rode one of four quarterly sections into which the larger route was divided.

Sometime in the fall of 1848, Beckwourth was riding south from Monterey to Dana's Ranch. As was common for riders along that stretch, he stopped to rest and water his horses at the former Spanish mission of San Miguel, which was then owned by a family named Reed. The mission, located on the Salinas River along the primary route to the gold mines in the north, served as a kind of inn, and Beckwourth had stopped there often. This time, what he found inside proved more terrifying to him than anything he had previously encountered in the course of his violent life.

It was dusk when he arrived, and he found it curious that no candles seemed to be burning inside the mission. Usually, too, one of the Reed's large playful dogs bounded out to greet him or at least raised a hullabaloo that announced his arrival, but that night all was still, except for the chirping of the crickets. He went inside, which smelled faintly of smoke, and shouted, but there was no response. In the kitchen, his foot stumbled over something; a body lay on the floor. A drunken guest, Beckwourth assumed, and gave the recumbent carcass a kick. The body did not move.

Beckwourth went outside to his horse, which he had left grazing in the mission's orchard, and removed two pistols from his saddlebag, then fashioned a torch from some wood he found on the ground. In the kitchen, the flickering firelight illuminated a bloody handprint on the adobe wall and a trail of blood leading from a wound in the skull of the man on the floor to the interior of the house. Creeping cautiously along, as silently as he ever made his way through a cottonwood thicket while fearing an Indian ambush, Beckwourth followed the trail through several silent rooms, until at last he reached the final horror: 11 more dead bodies, 2 of them small children, stacked like cordwood. All had been shot, had their throats slit, or their skulls bashed in. The assassins had been planning to burn them when something—perhaps Beckwourth's arrival—scared them off.

They were not the only ones who were frightened. Beckwourth raced outside to the orchard, jumped on his horse, and set off for the military garrison at Monterey at full gallop. Years later, the officer in charge there, Lieutenant William Tecumseh Sherman, still vividly recalled Beckwourth arriving, his spent but still game mount kicking up dust with every stride:

> "Leftenant, they killed them all, not even sparing the baby." With an earnestness not to be mistaken, he reiterated: "Leftenant, I tell you that Reed at San Miguel is killed, all his family and servants, not excepting the baby." He then told me, with a vividness not exceeded by Dickens, how he had received his mail at Dana's, had ridden on to San Luis Obispo, and so on to San Miguel. . . . The whole scene was so horrid that Jim Beckworth, though he spent his whole life with Indians and hunters, confessed that he was *scared*, that he regained his horse down in the orchard, and did not stop until he reached me, ninety miles away at Monterey.

A detachment of soldiers, under the command of Lieutenant E. O. C. Ord was sent to San Miguel, where they found the carnage Beckwourth had described and the mission to have been robbed. After a short search, they captured the murderers, who were executed by firing squad at Santa Barbara.

Sherman, who would go on to become one of the greatest military figures in U.S. history, held a rather different opinion of Beckwourth, whom he dealt with on many other occasions less dramatic than the Reed murders, than did many of his contemporaries. Although acknowledging that Beckwourth's "reputation for veracity was not good," Sherman believed him to be "one of the best chroniclers of events on the plains that I have ever encountered." The soldier was as confused as everyone else about Beckwourth's racial identity, however; he believed him to be a "cross" between a Crow Indian and a French-Canadian voyageur.

California in the gold rush days was a good place for an enterprising not-so-young-anymore man, especially one with the variety of irregular skills that Beckwourth had acquired in the course of his venturesome days. After several more months as a dispatch rider, Beckwourth resigned. He rambled all about the new state, surfacing at a number of the boomtowns and shanty cities that had sprung up as a result of the influx of the gold-hungry forty-niners come west to seek their fortune. One week he was in San Francisco, the next in Stockton, the next in Sonora, several weeks after that in a mining hamlet called Mormon Bar on the American River. He relied on a variety of stratagems to put money in his pocket, where it never stayed for very long: dealing and playing cards, a little prospecting, guiding greenhorns to likely gold strikes, horse rustling.

It was a boom-or-bust existence, mirroring the economic life of the state. For example, after a successful night at the gaming tables in Stockton—where a dozen card tables were set up under the awnings of the stores on Main Street as soon as the sun went down, Mexican blankets were spread out in the dust surrounding them to accomodate the overflow demand, and the gambling lasted until dawn—Beckwourth might find his saddlebags overflowing with gold and silver coins; two days' carousing in Sacramento later, his pockets would be bare. When down-and-out, he often swapped a yarn for a meal; his enthralled listeners invariably felt that they had gotten the better part of the deal.

The most revealing look at Beckwourth at this time was provided by John Letts, the proprietor of a

"Jim Beckwourth," said Lieutenant William Tecumseh Sherman, the officer in charge of the military garrison at Monterey, California, in 1848, "was, in my estimate, one of the best chroniclers of events on the plains that I have encountered, though his reputation for veracity was not good." Sherman rose from his post to become one of the top generals in the U.S. Army and a pivotal figure in the Civil War.

Prospectors pan for precious metal during the California gold rush in the mid-19th century. Beckwourth drifted across the state in the late 1840s and most of the 1850s, earning money by gambling, horse rustling, and serving as a guide, as well as by prospecting.

general store in Mormon Bar. In that capacity, Letts met a large number of "strange adventurers . . . who have as great an aversion to law and civilization as they have to the manacles of a prison," but none was as unforgettable as Beckwourth. He galloped up to the store one fine spring morning, a "strange-looking being" mounted on a gray horse, wrapped in a poncho, a rifle over one shoulder, wearing elkskin leggings, Mexican spurs and boots, and a rather battered sombrero. A friend of Letts's named Tracy, who with the proprietor was sunning himself on the store's front porch, recognized the "old mountaineer" from his days in Santa Fe. He greeted the newcomer with a question that Beckwourth often heard: "Hey, Jim, whose horse is that?"

"How do I know whose horse it is?" Beckwourth replied.

"Well, where did you get him?"

"I stole him from an Indian, of course." Where-upon Beckwourth announced that he was hungry and penniless. He must have especially enjoyed Letts's flapjacks and bacon, for he treated his host and his friend to his entire life story, which Letts described as a "most exciting romance, interspersed with thrilling adventures and 'hair-breadth 'scapes.'" Beckwourth included his days with the Crow and some boastful accounts of his prowess as a horse thief, in which capacity he claimed he had been hired by the U.S. Army to bedevil the Mexicans in California and New Mexico.

Letts recorded that Beckwourth was a mixture of "the negro, Indian, and Anglo-Saxon blood," although it is unclear whether he believed Beckwourth was part black because his guest told him as much, because of his "copper complexion," or because his Santa Fe friend passed on the knowledge. Other Californians whom Beckwourth regaled with his history at about this time recalled that he told them either that he was a Frenchman or descended from an English lord.

After a couple of days, Beckwourth rode on, and Letts assumed he would never see him again, but three weeks later he returned, riding the same gray horse. He entered the store and tossed a handkerchief filled with silver pieces—the proceeds from some successful gambling upriver—on the counter and insisted that Letts keep it as repayment for his hospitality. "Money," wrote Letts about Beckwourth, "was an incumbrance to which he would not submit. . . . Sometimes he would win several thousand dollars in one night, and the next night he would have every man drunk in town; what he could not spend in drink, he would give to the poor, or to his friends."

That night in Mormon Bar, Beckwourth enjoyed another fantastic run at the card tables; Letts last saw him at midnight mounting "Old Gray" with "as much money as he could conveniently carry"—close to $20,000—bound for Sacramento. A traveler reported to the storekeeper the next day that he had seen Beckwourth asleep under a tree, using his bulging moneybag as a pillow. ✿

9

THE ENDLESS TRAIL

JIM BECKWOURTH'S ARRIVAL in Sacramento was the occasion for a spectacular citywide binge that was the talk of the town for months afterward. As John Letts relates, "He had all the inhabitants drunk who were disposed that way . . . and one week after his advent, he had *invested* his last dollar."

Sometime earlier, Beckwourth had signed on with the army to make a mail delivery to Santa Fe; unfortunately, according to Letts, the "time arrived while he was *entertaining* the city." The result was a rip-roaring saloon brawl with the officers sent to remind him of his responsibility and a short stint in the city lockup. Such stays, said Letts, were always "sufficient to bring him to his senses, and make him long for his mountain air." The last Letts heard of Beckwourth, he had resumed his work in the "horse trade."

That work continued to take him into the rich valleys on the California side of the Sierra Nevada. Sometime in the winter of 1850, Beckwourth discovered a pass through the mountains that could be easily traversed by the covered wagons, carrying pioneers, that were then crossing Nevada's arid Great Basin for California in great number. Travelers along what would soon be known as the Beckwourth Trail

Cathedral Forest *by Albert Bierstadt. For travelers who journeyed into northern California from a region north of Reno, Nevada, their arduous passage across rugged terrain was abetted by Beckwourth's discovery of the Beckwourth Trail in 1850.*

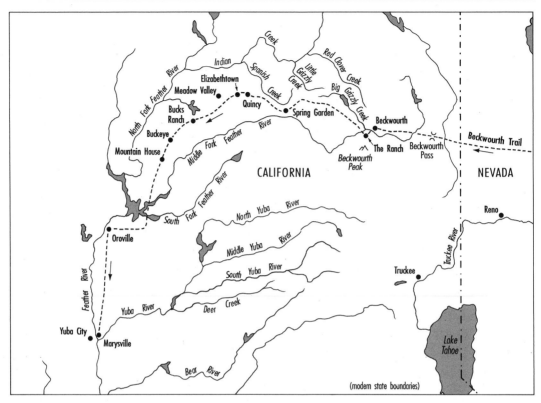

The Beckwourth Trail, which the frontiersman discovered in northern California. Beckwourth established a hotel, ranch, and trading post where Grizzly Creek meets Feather River.

crossed the Humboldt Sink area of the Great Basin, forded the Truckee River as it wended south from Pyramid Lake, then continued west through the mountains via Beckwourth Pass, on to the pleasant and fertile valleys along the Middle Fork of the Feather River and such burgeoning settlements as Marysville and Oroville.

Beckwourth established a combination ranch, trading post, and hotel along the trail, in the stunningly beautiful valley, named after himself, where Grizzly Creek meets the Middle Fork of the Feather. According to the discoverer of the pass, his was the only home between the valley and the Great Salt Lake. From the ranch, he would ride out along the trail and through the mountains to meet the pioneers' wagons in Nevada and guide them through "his" pass and into California. For these services, he was presumably paid both by the prospective settlers and the new municipalities in the region, all of them eager to attract new residents.

The Beckwourth Trail became one of the most commonly used pioneer routes from the Great Basin to California. In 1855, for example, 10,000 emigrants' wagons came through Beckwourth Pass. Yet its discoverer's generosity apparently kept his business from being as lucrative as it might have been. Granville Stuart was one of many California pioneers whose family and animals found food, shelter, a resting place, and excellent conversation at the Beckwourth Ranch, which became known as the "emigrant's landing place." Stuart said of Beckwourth that his "nature was a hospitable and generous one, and he supplied the pressing necessities of starving emigrants, often without money—they agreeing to pay him later, which I regret to say, many of them failed to do."

Beckwourth himself said that "numbers have put up at my ranch without a morsel of food, and without a dollar in the world to procure any. They never were refused what they asked for at my house. . . . I cannot find it in my heart to refuse relief to such necessities, and if my pocket suffers a little, I have my recompense in a feeling of internal satisfaction."

Those who stopped at the Beckwourth Ranch had their spirits lifted as well as their bellies filled. Virtually all whose recollections survive mention being greatly entertained by Beckwourth's tales. To these newcomers to the Far West, there was no question that Beckwourth was the real thing, the quintessential mountain man. Many remembered his facility with a variety of Indian languages, others that he fed them elk and bear meat from animals he had killed himself.

Ina Coolbrith, who was a very young girl when her family came to California via the Beckwourth

Trail, remembered a quality of his not frequently mentioned: gentleness. To the young pioneer, Beckwourth was "one of the most beautiful creatures that ever lived. He was rather dark and wore his hair in two long braids, twisted with colored cord that gave him a picturesque appearance. He wore a leather coat and moccasins and rode a horse without a saddle. . . When Jim Beckwourth said he would like to have my mother's little girls ride into California on his horse in front of him, I was the happiest little girl in the world. After two or three days of heavy riding, we came at last in sight of California and there on the boundary Jim Beckwourth stopped, and pointing forward, said, 'Here is California, little girls, here is your kingdom.'"

Another young woman who traveled the trail with her family remembered there being much laughter, music, and storytelling at the Beckwourth Ranch and that when they parted company Beckwourth presented her father with his photograph.

A somewhat more unusual individual spent the winter of 1854 as Beckwourth's guest at the ranch. Thomas D. Bonner, known to history as T.D., qualified as a bona fide character even by the outsized standards of the Old West. A monumental drunkard and an infamous confidence man, he had come to California in headlong flight from the heartbreak and disgrace of his life in Massachusetts, where his drinking and flagrant disregard of his responsibilities had contributed to the premature death of his wife and several children. Following these tragedies, Bonner, a self-styled poet and journalist, eked out a living as a temperance crusader, writing and publishing a number of pamphlets, broadsides, and poems condemning the evils of demon rum, a career that reached its peak when he became the publisher of a newspaper in Pittsfield, Massachusetts.

A view of Denver, Colorado, around 1860, when Beckwourth operated a store just north of the growing city. After the store had begun to attract a number of Cheyenne as customers, he went to work for them as an Indian agent.

The *New England Cataract*, with its motto of Protect the Fallen—and Punish the Tempter printed above the masthead, was one of the more unique journals in the history of Pittsfield County. According to one contemporary historian, "It was grossly personal and scurrilous in its expression" of Bonner's antialcohol views, which won its offices the honor of being overrun and ransacked one night by an irate mob, the "only instance of that kind in the history of the Berkshires." The mob tossed the paper's printing press and its other equipment into a lake and chased Bonner from town. He bounced around the Northeast for a couple of more years, penning and publishing maudlin temperance ballads, before surfacing in California at about the time of the gold rush.

Out west, Bonner for the first time combined his two former pastimes of drinking and temperance crusading, chattering incessantly to any who would listen about the temptation of the grape and the ruin of his own life and earning a well-justified reputation as a prodigious boozer. A balding, fat-faced, gray-eyed fellow, round as a beer barrel, mild mannered and soft-spoken, with a double chin imperfectly masked by a satanic goatee, he became infamous in the mining towns as the "peregrinating justice," a confidence man who would manage to win election as justice of the peace, then enrich himself on the outrageous "court fees" he charged. Bonner, who often held court in a saloon, charged fees to bring a lawsuit, fees to drop one, fees of the victorious party, and even fees of a witness to testify. According to one who knew him, his decisions were informed by a rather singular theory of jurisprudence: "It was customary for him to decide against the party whom he thought was best able to pay the costs. Good business principles would not permit him to do otherwise."

For a time, Bonner would be able to get by with his outrageous conduct, for many towns preferred even a scoundrel as judge to the utter lawlessness that was then so prevalent. But Bonner's transgressions would inevitably become so outrageous that he would be forced to decamp, carried by the trusty mule on which he made his erratic way.

Somewhere in the course of his own carousing, Beckwourth made the acquaintance of the Squire, as the roistering Bonner was sometimes known. At Bonner's suggestion—there was a considerable market in the East for "true-life" western literature— they agreed to collaborate on Beckwourth's life story. So throughout the winter months of 1854, as he had done so many times before, Beckwourth told his tales of high adventure, narrow escape, reckless heroism, and thoughtless cruelty, of friendship and betrayal, of the beauty of the wilderness and its inevitable destruction, while his bibulous ghostwriter scribbled frantically to get it all down.

The publication of *The Life and Adventures of James P. Beckwourth, Mountaineer, Scout, Pioneer, and*

Chief of the Crow Nation in 1856 by Harper Brothers earned its subject a good deal of renown and resentment; even more criticism for its truthfulness, or lack thereof, which has continued to the present day; and not a cent in advance monies or royalties, which his coauthor apparently pocketed for himself. After the completion of their book, Beckwourth never again heard from Bonner, who went back east to arrange its publication. The last history records of the Squire is a tawdry 1861 incident in which he was charged with stealing a cask of rum from a store in Lynn, Massachusetts, where he was serving as night watchman.

His book's publication made Beckwourth something of a celebrity (as well as a target for resentful, racist, or humorless contemporaries and historians), and people frequently came to the ranch, which was now the seat of a small community of about 20 homes, just to get a glimpse of this western legend. Obed Wilson, one such visitor, described an orderly "plantation" with "fields of fine vegetables, a herd of about two hundred sheep, a hundred ponies and immense flocks of domestic fowl." Its proprietor, as becomes a legend nearing 60, was looking somewhat "worn and broken, but his large muscular frame seemed still sound and capable of great endurance."

Beckwourth Ranch would seem to have been a comfortable haven for an aging mountain man, but in 1858 Beckwourth abandoned it. Various reasons are given: He was chased off by a committee of vigilantes investigating reports that he built his admirable herd of ponies through theft; he bet all that he owned, including the ranch, on a footrace he tried to rig, only to be outsmarted. But in all likelihood he decided that it was simply time to try something else.

The arrival of this mountain-man celebrity in various cities over the next couple of years invariably attracted the attention of the press. In St. Louis, in

August 1859, Beckwourth complained to a reporter that he no longer knew the city of his youth and had to hire a guide to show him around. In Kansas City a month later, he was hailed as the "great western guide and interpreter." In Denver, where Beckwourth arrived in November, the editor of the *Rocky Mountain News* wrote he was pleased to discover that the "old mountaineer" was a "polished gentleman, possessing a fund of general information which few can boast." Based, perhaps, on the harsh, in part racially based criticisms of Beckwourth that had already begun to circulate, the newspaperman had expected a "rough, illiterate backwoodsman."

Beckwourth settled in Denver, but his stay there was not to be very happy, for the West that he had known was on the verge of vanishing forever. A boomtown created by the onrush of prospectors to the Rockies in search of gold, Denver had not even existed when Beckwourth first went to California, and he was able to see that the tenuous coexistence that had existed among trappers, traders, and Indians in his heyday was about to give way in Colorado to a war of extermination in the face of large-scale settlement.

The same pattern was soon to prevail elsewhere beyond the Mississippi. Within a couple of years, Congress would pass legislation providing for the construction of the transcontinental railroad and granting free homestead tracts of 160 acres to western settlers willing to farm such land for five years. The onrush of American settlement would leave little room for the Indians, and a concerted effort would be made to drive them from their lands and to uproot and destroy their culture.

Emblematic of both the passing of Jim Beckwourth's West and the end of the way of life of the Plains Indians was the devastation of the vast buffalo herds that had once roamed the West. Because the great herds impeded the construction of the railroads and provided the Indians with spiritual and physical sustenance—as food, as shelter, as clothing, and as an element of religious worship—the buffalo was hunted relentlessly by American hunters, with the express purpose of bringing about its extinction and thereby hastening the demise of the Indians. An estimated 60 million of the shaggy horned beasts roamed North America when Europeans first began to settle on the continent; by 1900, only 300 would remain.

Beckwourth's sympathy was with the Cheyenne, who were bearing the brunt of the desire of Colorado pioneers for land. In his autobiography, he had decried the use of troops against the "innocent" Indians, and now he felt like "prosecuting the settlers," he told a Denver journalist, for the city's outlying sections rested on his former hunting grounds. The store he soon opened just north of the city, in a suburb called Highland, became a regular stopping place for Cheyenne coming to Denver to trade, and he became an unofficial spokesman for their grievances, which in addition to American encroachment upon their lands included mistreatment—rape, robbery, and murder—upon their forays to town. "All our Indian troubles," Beckwourth, who by then had been appointed acting Indian agent, wrote in a letter to the *Rocky Mountain News*, "are produced by the imprudent acts of unprincipled white men."

The certainty that his time was passing only added to the usual dispiritedness that pursued Beckwourth when he attempted to live a settled existence. He married again and fathered a daughter, but the girl died in infancy. There were a number of unseemly incidents—public drunkenness, a charge of stealing from an army post, a trial for manslaughter following the shooting of an acquaintance. (Beckwourth was acquitted of the slaying, mostly on the grounds that the dead man had instigated their argument and that by killing him he had rid the city of a public nuisance.) A fall from a horse slowed him down.

Correspondence with Jim Bridger and a resumption of his friendship and business relationship with Louis Vasquez provided reason for cheer, but the deteriorating relations between the settlers and the Cheyenne continued to worry him. Then, in late November 1864, sometime near Thanksgiving, one of Colonel John Chivington's patrols rousted Beckwourth from bed, and he was made to help guide the cavalry to the Cheyenne and Arapaho encampment at Sand Creek.

In contrast with his usual utterances, both spoken and verbal, Beckwourth's testimony before a military committee of inquiry investigating the Sand Creek massacre was straightforward, as if the horrors he had witnessed spoke for themselves, with no need of embellishment or added emphasis. His account of the death of the trusting White Antelope was typical. When asked the name of the Indian whom Beckwourth had testified tried to speak with Chivington to prevent the massacre, Beckwourth replied: "The name he went by with the Indians was Spotted Antelope, and by the whites, White Antelope. He came running out to meet the command at the time the battle had commenced, holding up his hands and saying 'Stop! Stop!' He spoke it in as plain English as I can. He stopped and folded his arms until shot down."

"Was any attention paid to White Antelope as he advanced toward the command?" one of the investigators asked.

"None, only to shoot him, as I saw," Beckwourth replied. He went on to add that two-thirds of the Indians killed at Sand Creek had been women and children.

A large mound of buffalo bones serves as testimony to the passing of Beckwourth's "howling wilderness." The abundant wildlife in the Old West had impeded American settlement by slowing railroad construction and providing sustenance to the Indians.

Heartsick and weary, bitter in the manner of a man who observes his world changing in ways he had never foreseen and too rapidly for him to comprehend, Beckwourth decided to return to the Cheyenne, only to find himself excluded as an outsider by a people as oppressed by a sense of their collective mortality as he was of his own. He found them in mid-January 1865, camped on the White Man's Fork of the Smoky Hill River. They were headed north, toward Nebraska or Wyoming.

As Beckwourth entered the lodge of Leg-in-the-Water, an old friend, the chief stood up and asked him, "Medicine Calf, what have you come here for; have you fetched the white man to finish killing our families again?"

Beckwourth asked him to assemble the tribal council, whom he then sought to persuade to live in peace with the whites, who were "as numerous as the leaves on the trees" and could never be defeated in battle.

"We know it," responded the Cheyenne elders. "But what do we want to live for? The white man has taken our country, killed all our game; was not satisfied with that, but killed our wives and children.

Now no peace. We want to go and meet our fathers in the spirit land. We loved the whites until we found out they lied to us, and robbed us of what we had. We have raised the battle-axe until death."

The Cheyenne then asked Beckwourth why he had "come to Sand Creek with the soldiers to show them the country," and he answered that he would have been hanged if he had not.

"Go and stay with your white brother," said the Indians, "but we are going to fight until the death."

So Beckwourth set back out on the trail, but it was almost at an end. He apparently spent some time with the army at Fort Laramie, most likely as a dispatch rider or a scout. Sometime in 1866, he entered into partnership with Jim Bridger in some sort of trading venture, the needs of which brought him back to his old haunts along the Bighorn River. There, according to George Templeton, an army lieutenant, Beckwourth passed away in early October 1866 from an unidentified illness while visiting the Crow.

But such a death would be unfitting for the old mountain man unless it had a story attached to it. According to persistent legend, Beckwourth's return to the Crow was the cause for great celebration. A huge banquet was held, and the village elders recounted all the tales of bravery and valor from the glorious times when Beckwourth had been their chief, before the soldiers had come to the mountains, before the Indians had become addicted to firewater, when the Crow were still a great people and their enemies still feared them. They asked him to become their chief once again, but he refused, graciously, explaining that he was tired and old. On the night before he was to leave, a great feast in his honor was held. The drums played, and the Indians danced, and Beckwourth was fed poison, for even in death he would be "good medicine."

It was possible that "I might return to them,"
Beckwourth had written of the Crow in the autobiography, "for there at least was fidelity, and, when my
soul should depart for the spirit land, their rude faith
would prompt them to paint my bones, and treasure
them until I should return from my ever-flowing
hunting grounds, and demand them at their hands."

The western press was more prosaic in announc-
ing his demise. "Jim Beckwith is dead," read the *Daily
Miners' Register* in February 1867. "At last the adventurous old mountaineer has succumbed to the penalty
which we must all pay, sooner or later. His life has
been one continuous chain of adventures. . . . His
last campaign settled him down among the mountains he had so often traversed as scout, guide, and
chief." The *Rocky Mountain News* recorded the com-
ments of his detractors, mentioning that phrases such
as "no loss to the country" and "it was about time"
were heard in the wake of the news of his death,
but continued on generously: "He doubtless had his
faults, and who has not? Certainly he was not worse
than any of us would likely have been with . . . such
surroundings through a long and eventful life."

Slave, free trapper; black, white, Indian; "gaudy
liar" and "one of the best chroniclers of events";
roughneck and gentleman; Indian killer and spokesman for their grievances; robber and generous bene-
factor; gleeful narrator of blood-soaked memoirs and
horrified witness to unprovoked massacre; historical
figure and legend of his own creation—Beckwourth
was all of these. Sometimes a liar, sometimes a
thief, maybe a scoundrel; redeemed by his generosity, good humor, imagination, always-abundant
courage, hunger for adventure, and unquenchable
thirst for freedom; Jim Beckwourth, if something less
than a hero, was never less than a representative
figure of his age, in all its contradictory, tumultuous,
and tragic glory.

CHRONOLOGY

--------●○●--------

ca. 1800   Born James Pierson Beckwith in Frederick County, Virginia

1808   Moves with his father, Jennings Beckwith, to a plantation at the Point, near St. Charles, Missouri

1810   Sent to school in St. Louis, Missouri

1819   Apprenticed to Casner and Sutton, a St. Louis smithy; quits apprenticeship after dispute; receives his legal manumission from Jennings Beckwith

ca. 1820   Travels to Fever River, Illinois (site of present-day Galena), to work in the lead mines

1823–24   Hires on as one of William Ashley's "enterprising young men," the free trappers of what would become the Rocky Mountain Fur Company

1825   Attends the first rendezvous of the mountain men, at Henry's Fork of the Green River, where he begins to establish a reputation as a masterful raconteur

1825–28   Traps along the Powder and Little Bighorn rivers

1828–29   "Taken captive" by the Crow Indians

1829–36   Becomes war chief of the Crow while simultaneously acting as agent of the American Fur Company; joins the Crow in numerous horse-stealing raids and battles

1837–38   Drives mules and carries messages for the U.S. Army in Florida during the Second Seminole War

1838–42   Works as a trader in various locations in Colorado and New Mexico; establishes a general store in Taos, New Mexico; marries Luisa Sandoval; helps found Pueblo, Colorado

1842–44   Leads trading expedition to California, where he participates in Bear Flag Rebellion; uses proceeds from horse thievery to purchase hotel in Santa Fe, New Mexico

1848   Discovers grisly murders at Dana's Ranch, California

1850   Discovers the Beckwourth Trail in the Sierra Nevada; builds ranch and trading post in Beckwourth Valley

1854   Dictates his memoirs to T. D. Bonner

1858–64   Leaves Beckwourth Ranch; settles in Denver, where he acts as Indian agent to the Cheyenne

1864   Unwillingly participates in massacre of the Arapaho and Cheyenne at Sand Creek, Colorado, on November 29

1865   Returns to the wilderness as a trader

1866   Dies in October while visiting the Crow along the Bighorn River

FURTHER READING

Allen, John Logan. *Jedediah Smith and the Mountain Men of the American West*. New York: Chelsea House, 1991.

Bartlett, Richard A., and William H. Goetzmann. *Exploring the American West: 1803–1879*. Washington, DC: National Park Service, 1982.

Beckwourth, James P., and T. D. Bonner. *The Life and Adventures of James P. Beckwourth, Mountaineer, Scout, Pioneer, and Chief of the Crow Nation*. 1856. Reprint. Lincoln: University of Nebraska Press, 1972.

De Voto, Bernard. *Across the Wide Missouri*. Boston: Houghton Mifflin, 1947.

———. *The Course of Empire*. Boston: Houghton Mifflin, 1952.

Gilbert, Bil. *The Trailblazers*. Alexandria, VA: Time-Life, 1973.

Katz, William Loren. *Black Indians: A Hidden Heritage*. New York: Atheneum, 1986.

———. *The Black West*. Seattle: Open Hand Publishing, 1987.

Lapp, Rudolph M. *Blacks in Gold Rush California*. New Haven: Yale University Press, 1977.

Lavender, David. *The Great West*. Boston: Houghton Mifflin, 1965.

Morgan, Dale L. *Jedediah Smith and the Opening of the West*. Lincoln: University of Nebraska Press, 1964.

Parkman, Francis, Jr. *The Oregon Trail*. 1849. Reprint. New York: Penguin, 1985.

Van Every, Dale. *The Final Challenge: The American Frontier 1804–1845*. New York: Penguin, 1985.

Wilson, Elinor. *Jim Beckwourth: Black Mountain Man, War Chief of the Crows, Trader, Trapper, Explorer, Frontiersman, Guide, Scout, Interpreter, Adventurer, and Gaudy Liar*. Norman: University of Oklahoma Press, 1972.

INDEX

PICTURE CREDITS

Among the Sierra Nevada Mountains California, by Albert Bierstadt, 1868, oil on canvas, National Museum of American Art/Art Resource: pp. 2–3; The Bettmann Archive: pp. 23, 60, 82–83, 85, 86, 97; *Cathedral Forest*, by Albert Bierstadt, oil on canvas/Art Resource: p. 100; Colorado Historical Society: pp. 3, 10, 12, 14, 17, 20, 47, 59, 67, 70, 79, 88, 93, 98, 105; *El Capitan, Yosemite Valley*, by Albert Bierstadt, oil on paper mounted on canvas/Art Resource: p. 26; *The Grand Canyon of the Yellowstone*, by Thomas Moran, 1893–1901, oil on canvas, National Museum/Art Resource: p. 43; H. Pollard Collection/National Archives of Alberta, Canada: p. 111; Library of Congress: p. 36 (neg. # LC-USZ622165); Missouri Historical Society: pp. 19, 30, 34, 40, 50, 54, 58, 72; *Mist in Kanab Canyon, Utah*, by Thomas Moran, 1892, oil on canvas, National Museum/Art Resource: p. 63; Nevada State Historical Society: pp. 38, 114; Utah State Historical Society: p. 56; Virginia Historical Society: p. 29 Maps (pp. 77, 102) by Gary Tong

SEAN DOLAN has a degree in literature and American history from SUNY Oswego. He is the author of many biographies and histories for young adult readers and has edited a series of volumes on the famous explorers of history.

NATHAN IRVIN HUGGINS, one of America's leading scholars in the field of black studies, helped select the titles for the BLACK AMERICANS OF ACHIEVEMENT series, for which he also served as senior consulting editor. He was the W.E.B. Du Bois Professor of History and of Afro-American Studies at Harvard University and the director of the W.E.B. Du Bois Institute for Afro-American Research at Harvard. He received his doctorate from Harvard in 1962 and returned there as a professor in 1980 after teaching at Columbia University, the University of Massachusetts, Lake Forest College, and the California State University, Long Beach. He was the author of four books and dozens of articles, including *Black Odyssey: The Afro-American Ordeal in Slavery*, *The Harlem Renaissance*, and *Slave and Citizen: The Life of Frederick Douglass*, and was associated with the Children's Television Workshop, National Public Radio, the Boston Athenaeum, the Museum of Afro-American History, the Howard Thurman Educational Trust, and Upward Bound. Professor Huggins died in 1989, at the age of 62, in Cambridge, Massachusetts.